UNITARIANISM DEFINED.

THE

SCRIPTURE DOCTRINE

OF THE

FATHER, SON AND HOLY GHOST.

A

COURSE OF LECTURES,

BY

FREDERICK A. FARLEY, D.D.,

PASTOR OF THE CHURCH OF THE SAVIOUR, BROOKLYN, N. Y.

BOSTON:

AMERICAN UNITARIAN ASSOCIATION.

MDCCCLXXIII.

Cambridge: Presswork by John Wilson and Son.

CONTENTS.

PREFACE.

THE following Lectures were delivered in the spring of 1859. They were not originally written out, but delivered orally after being carefully studied, as an advocate at the Bar speaks from his "brief." When, therefore, I was requested by my congregation—in a spirit which made my duty plain—to publish them, I found myself, should I comply, quite likely to disappoint any readers who heard them, by at least the loss they might feel of that more fresh and vivacious manner, which belongs to extemporaneous speech. Much as the old dame felt, who, when asked to sign a request to her Pastor for a copy of a sermon for the press: "La!" said she, "it's no use: you may print the *sarmon*, but you can't print the *tone!*" And in truth, "the tone" is of some importance, even if it be not the best in the world. The Lectures had to be written out from the *brief;* the excitement of a large and earnest audience was gone; the matter had been in a considerable degree dismissed from my mind; and it was very much like beginning to do over again in cold blood what had been done in a glow. I confess, therefore, to some reluctance at first to setting about the necessary preparation for the press. But circumstances conspired to urge me: circumstances which seemed at once to create and to indicate a fresh demand in the community, for a re-presentation of the grounds on which a faith, to me inestimably precious, rests. My own deep love and gratitude for the faith which has been baptized with the name of Unitarianism; my conviction of its being the original and essential faith of the New Testament and the primitive Church, and destined yet to recover its hold upon the affections and the allegiance of Christendom; my persuasion that it is altogether without warrant either to denounce or regard as infidel that vast majority of our population which is now unhappily dissociated from all the religious institutions of this nominally Christian land—since among the portion of it most indifferent or most opposed to the orthodox dispensation of the Gospel, many might be found ready to accept, could they only be brought to understand, our more rational and Scriptural views; my observation, notwithstanding the wide-spread and deep-seated popular prejudice against Unitarianism, of the increasing influence of its principles of interpretation of the Scriptures, of its mode of regarding the Scriptures themselves, and of its essential and peculiar spirit, upon the general tone of religious thought and discussion ; have all urged and helped me on.

The *name*, Unitarianism, I care little for in itself, though I like it as sufficiently apt and distinctive, where and so long as a distinction must be made ; and while I see the *thing* which it denotes doing its work, and leavening the mass, however unacknowledged or unobserved even, by those whom it is doing perhaps the most to bless—yes, doing the work of orthodoxy, and by degrees winning its prestige—I am content. By *name*, I never expected to see it go with a rush ; but since I have been able to note the current of religious thought, and especially since the great controversy more than thirty years ago, in Europe, in Great Britain, and at home, tending to and largely resulting in more liberal views and a more liberal spirit in the very bosom of the orthodox churches ; to see how these pervade the best literature of the age—how they are enlarging the bounds within which men of different names and sects can co-operate for the truest Christianization of society and the world—how they are driving intolerance and bigotry back into the skulking-places of mere ignorance and superstition—I feel sure, that all that *we* have been most ready to contend for under that *name*, was never more active or mighty. The practical recognition of the great truths, not merely of One God, but of One God, the FATHER—of One all-sufficient Saviour, the Saviour of all, and not of an "elect" portion of the race only—of the Holy Spirit of our Father in heaven, the Comforter ever ready to come into the hearts of all who seek it—of the brotherhood of man, in which all the great interests of the race are seen to be inseparably one, and as such to be regarded and cared for by the Church of Christ more than any or all matters of creed or belief—these among the leading truths, which Unitarianism has always held dear and has always faithfully contended for, apart from all metaphysical subtleties and confusion of tongues, were never more emphasized than now in the Christian consciousness, whatever the loyalty, professed in any quarter, to symbols and confessions in effect fast growing obsolete.

The necessity of the case has compelled me to a more rigid adherence to purely dogmatic statement and discussion, than I could have wished. Believing, as I do, in Christianity as an Authoritative, Revealed Religion, and that it still suffers from corruptions induced by false glosses and interpretations of its Records, I am unfeignedly anxious to commend it in its simplicity to the serious and devout inquirer. Not that I do not believe, on the one hand, that a Calvinist, or a Trinitarian of any stamp, and, on the other, that a Deist, a Naturalist, a Rationalist, may be as good as—perhaps better than—many who boast most loudly of their Christian faith; but that God, having seen fit to reveal his will through his Son, it is my bounden duty, as one to whom it has come, not only to see to it that I understand aright, accept, and obey that Revelation, just as it is; but as one of its Ministers, aid others to do the same.

If any think such Lectures are not needed, because orthodoxy has in many quarters, or in many respects been ameliorated, it remains true that even the most liberal orthodox bodies or churches still retain their old Symbols, Catechisms, and Confessions of Faith; and that by these in by far the overwhelming majority of cases, is a man's fitness to be or become a member of the Christian Church, tested. So long as such is the fact, so long must these discussions have place.

The words *orthodox* and *orthodoxy*, are of course used throughout the volume, as merely designating the popular faith, or the faith professed by the majority. I have also often introduced "concessions of Trinitarians"; not, surely, because Trinitarian expositions or criticisms are in themselves of more weight than those of our own household of faith, but because they are in the nature of attestations from the opposite side of the argument, in every given case, to the strength of our position. Is it sufficiently known, that the entire Unitarian argument may be sustained by the "concessions" of Trinitarian expositors and critics, in reference to every point of Scripture, and the History of the Church?*

It will at once be seen, that I plant myself upon the Bible, and especially the New Testament of our Lord and Saviour Jesus Christ. I hold, that a just interpretation is needed to bring out the spirit from beneath the letter. I believe in progress; but in religious matters, progress within Christianity, not outside or beyond it. The Gospel is specially the religion of progress; has always been, and will always be in advance of the highest religious growth of man. To leave it, would be only religiously to retrograde. Progress? Yes. But remember

* Let my readers consult that remarkable volume of John Wilson, entitled, "Concessions of Trinitarians," published in England, in 1842; and his "Unitarian Principles confirmed by Trinitarian Testimonies," 2d vol. of the "Theological Library" of the American Unitarian Association, Boston, 1855.

that some things are fixed, permanent facts. No more light is to be looked for upon them. They are no longer matters of debate to the Christian mind. GOD IS. He is ONE. JESUS is the CHRIST—there is no other; and he is the All-sufficient Saviour and Son of God. Man, too, is immortal, and the subject of a righteous retribution. Here are examples of what I deem fixed, settled facts, and no longer in my own mind even debateable.

Finally—as to the importance of the questions herein discussed. Surely, if God exist in Three co-equal, co-eternal Persons, each God, each the object of worship—if JESUS CHRIST be verily GOD, the proper object of man's highest homage and adoration—we must desire to know and to confess it. To be ignorant of, when I might know it—to deny, when I ought to confess it—were indeed taking a tremendous risk. But on the other hand, if it be not so—if God be One, without admixture of Persons—One Person only; if the FATHER alone be GOD; if He alone is to be supremely worshipped; if Jesus Christ be not GOD—not the object, therefore, of divine worship—not Him in whom we live and move and have our being—then, with my present convictions that all this is true, what gross idolatry—"accounting or worshipping that for God which is not God"*—would it be in me to worship and adore His Son? And what the position of our Trinitarian brethren, should they be finally proved unfaithful to the light?

*South.

LECTURES.

LECTURE I.

THE UNITY OF GOD—THE TRINITY.

If any doctrine can be called fundamental to Revealed Religion, it must be that of the strict, simple, unqualified Unity of God. I take this to be universally admitted, nay, insisted on. There is not a more obvious truth in the Scriptures; none more coïncident with their whole tenor and drift, or with their most express and positive declarations. Rightly interpreted, rightly understood, there is not even an intimation or hint of any thing else. The language of the Bible upon this point is every where plain and explicit. The declaration recorded in the fourth verse of the sixth chapter of Deuteronomy, then so solemnly made to the people of Israel through Moses; and afterwards in the coming in of the new and better dispensation, quoted and so emphatically affirmed by our Lord Jesus Christ in the twenty-ninth verse of the twelfth chapter of St. Mark's Gospel—"Hear, O Israel, the Lord thy God is One Lord"—is clear and indisputable. Unitarians, therefore, not only without hesitation, but in perfect harmony with the unambiguous language of Scripture, and on the express authority of Christ himself, affirm that God is One; in the strictest meaning of the word, One; One Person, One Being, One intelligent, conscious Mind. There are seventeen texts in the New Testament alone, in which He is expressly called the One or Only God. In thirteen hundred passages the word God occurs; in not one of them is there any necessary implication, but directly the contrary, of a plurality of Persons in the Godhead. In but very few of them has it ever been pretended that such a plurality is even implied.

Indeed, I know not, had the sacred writers proposed to guard against any different belief from that of the simple Unity of God, how their testimony on this point could have been more express. Besides the citation just made from one of the Gospels, St. Paul, in the eighth chapter of his first Epistle to the Corinthians, having declared that "there is none other God but One," in the same breath adds, "to us there is One God, the Father"—to US, Christians, that One God is the Father. So in the fourth chapter of his Epistle to the Ephesians he says: "There is One God and Father of all, who is above all." In perfect correspondence with all this, we find in the nineteenth chapter of St. Matthew's Gospel that our Lord, when a man addressed him with the words "*Good* Master," declined the epithet; saying: "Why callest thou me good? There is none Good but One, that is, God."

Thus clearly is the fact that God is One, strictly and only One, stated in Scripture. But that this One God is the Father—in other words, that the Father, and the Father only, is this One God, is just as clear. The beloved Apostle John has recorded at length a most remarkable prayer, offered by our Lord when he was about to leave the world. If he would ever have spoken simply, unequivocally, according to his convictions, nay, his knowledge, it must have been at that solemn hour, in that most solemn act. Hear him, then, addressing the FATHER: "This is Life Eternal, that they might know THEE, the ONLY TRUE GOD—and Jesus Christ whom Thou hast sent."* Could any language be more explicit than this?

Omniscience is an attribute essential to Supreme Deity; but to this, Christ not only makes no pretensions, he disclaims it in an emphatic manner when he says: "Of that day and that hour knoweth no man; no, not the angels who are in heaven; neither the Son; but the Father."† In the parallel passage in Matthew‡ he says most expressly, "but my Father ONLY." No resort can here be had, as has been attempted by Trinitarians, to their favorite hypothesis — that merest hypothesis, that shallowest assumption, as I hope hereafter to show—namely, the Double Nature, or, as it is technically and theologically called, the Hypostatic Union; according to which Christ is both God and man. Whenever attempted, the conclusion has been only the more palpably impotent. The obvious difficulty of the text, on the supposition of the truth of the doctrine of the Trinity, cannot be overcome "by supposing that our Lord spake of himself here only

* John 17: 3. † Mark 13: 32. ‡ 24: 36.

as a man." For as the *orthodox* Macknight says*: "The name *Father* following that of *Son*, shows that he spake of himself as the Son of God, and not as the Son of man. Besides, the gradation in the sentence seems to forbid this solution. For the Son being mentioned after the angels, and immediately before the Father, is thereby declared to be more excellent than they, which he is not in respect of his human nature; and therefore he cannot be supposed to speak of himself in that nature."

Macknight here recognizes the ordinary Trinitarian idea, that the phrase or title "Son of God" implies the Divine Nature of our Lord, as "Son of Man" his Human Nature. Suppose, then, that our Lord was conscious of being possessed of this Double Nature; and that he actually meant what Trinitarians say he meant, that as "Son of God" he was God the Son, the second Person of the Godhead, and that as "Son of Man" he was indeed "*the* man," preëminently the man, but nevertheless man only, having, as they often allege, a human body and a human soul; how stands the case? Assuredly, his language, as recorded by St. Mark, must then be understood to admit, nay, with emphasis to declare his ignorance both as man and as God, both in his human and in his divine nature, "of that day and hour." If ignorant in that respect, if ignorant on any one, and but one point, he was not Omniscient. And I cannot help adding, though not discussing that topic now, that if in his divine nature, if as God the Son, he was not Omniscient, then that

* Harmony, Sec. 123.

divine nature was not the highest; then, as God the Son he was not the Supreme; he was God only in an inferior and subordinate sense, or as he himself, on another occasion, expressed it, as being one "to whom the word of God came."*

The argument is not weakened by reading "*no one*" instead of "*no man*" in the first clause, as the Greek might at least with equal correctness be rendered. For the words "the Son" are still there; they still stand in full force, used by Christ himself to distinguish himself from the Father, whom he describes as "the ONLY TRUE GOD"; while the expression "no one" is so sweeping of itself as to carry with it all other beings, even if none of them were specified, and unless some were excepted. One glorious exception, as we have seen, *is* made—"the Father only." The Father alone being Omniscient, is GOD alone and supreme.

The frequency with which God is called or described as "the Father," is also in this connection to be borne in mind. In the New Testament He is called simply "the Father" in no less than one hundred and twenty-two passages; in nineteen, "God the Father"; in various places, "God our Father," "Our Father," "God, even our Father," "God, even the Father," "Father of Mercies," or merciful Father, "Father of Glory," or glorious Father. He is declared in express terms to be "the God and Father of our Lord Jesus Christ"; while our Lord himself described Him as "your Father which is in heaven," "thy Father,"

* John 10 : 35.

"your Heavenly Father," "your Father"; and after his Resurrection, directed Mary to say to his disciples: "I ascend unto my Father and your Father, to my God and your God." Never in Scripture, not in one solitary instance, is there the phrase God the Son—which is so familiar to our ears that its profanity passes unnoticed.

Then the Father is the only object of supreme religious worship. Christ worshipped and prayed to the Father; and when asked by his disciples to teach them to pray, begins the form which he gave them with the invocation—"Our Father who art in Heaven." To the woman of Samaria he declared—mark the words—"The hour cometh and now is, when *the true worshippers* shall worship the Father." His precepts and his example were uniform and harmonious on this point. He always directed his followers to "pray to the Father," as he always himself prayed. Alluding to the time when he should be taken from them and go to the Father, he expressly forbids them from praying to himself, and points them to the Father. "In that day ye shall ask *me* nothing: verily, verily, I say unto you, whatsoever ye shall *ask of the Father* in my name, He will give it you."* One might almost suppose the Saviour had in view that gross corruption of Christian worship, in which he, and not *the* Father—*his* Father—is the Deity adored. Hence the constant practice of the Apostles, as may be seen throughout the Book of Acts and the Epistles. Nowhere do they pray, or teach to pray, to Christ.†

* John 16 : 23. † See e. g. Ephes. 3 : 14, etc.; ibid. 5 : 20; Col. 1 : 3.

Now, in direct opposition to this great, fundamental doctrine of the simple Unity of God, the vast majority of the Christian Church accepts, and for long centuries has accepted, the mysterious, irrational, unscriptural dogma of a Trinity of Persons in the Godhead. But not only is the dogma unscriptural, which is our cardinal objection to it, the very term "Trinity" is not of Scriptural derivation; and, as all who are familiar with the Scriptures know, is not to be found there, nor any word or term corresponding to it. The word first occurs in its Greek form (τριάς) in the writings of Theophilus, Bishop of Antioch, near the close of the second century; but even there it is not in the ecclesiastical sense in which the word was afterwards and is now used.* In its Latin form, (*Trinitas*,) with a more comprehensive doctrinal import, it is first found in Tertullian, a Presbyter of Carthage in Africa, who flourished about the same time; and from whom it seems to have been at once adopted by his pupil Cyprian and by Novatian.†

To justify the epithets which I have applied to the doctrine, let us look at some of the popular statements and expositions of it. I beg especial attention to the fact, not simply how various and often astounding in themselves are these statements and expositions, but how dissimilar to the language of Scripture—that Scripture which those churches and divines who make them, hold to be plenarily inspired; and, so far as they

* Theoph. ad Autol. ii. 15, cited by Hagenbach, Hist. of Doctrines; Buch's Translation, i. 128, note 2; Muenscher Dogm. Hist., Murdoch's Trans. p. 55.

† Hagenbach, id. note 3.

are Protestants, to be the sufficient rule of faith as well as practice. One would think that a scriptural doctrine or truth could be expressed in the language of Scripture; a Christian doctrine or truth, in the language of the Christian Scripture, "the New Testament of our Lord and Saviour Jesus Christ." To do this with the Trinity, is simply impossible, and therefore never attempted. Recourse must of necessity be had, not to "words which the Holy Ghost but which man's wisdom teacheth."

Turn then to the Liturgy of the Episcopal Church. In its First "Article of Religion" it declares: "In unity of the Godhead there be three persons, of one substance, power, and eternity, the Father, the Son, and the Holy Ghost."*

* The Episcopal Church in this country, did not attain uniformity of worship, till seven years after the war of the Revolution. Just two years after the Treaty of Paris, by which our national Independence was secured, the first Convention of that Church was held in Philadelphia, in September, 1785. Besides other omissions and alterations from the Liturgy of the English Established Church, to which the churches represented in this Convention had of course belonged, it reduced the number of the "Articles of Religion" from thirty-nine to twenty; struck out entire the Nicene and the Athanasian, and the clause, "He descended into Hell," from the Apostles' Creed; and, by a Special Committee, published the Prayer-Book in this form. This was a remarkable testimony to the then state of feeling and opinion in that Church, honestly and openly given. For although no essential difference may be detected as to points of faith between the *twenty* and the *thirty-nine* articles, there must have been some good reason for such a marked departure from the Liturgy of the Church of England as the rejection of two of its three Creeds; retaining the one which has so very little in it to be objected to—except its *name*, and that is not *in* it but *of* it, giving the false impression that it is the work of the Apostles, which notoriously it is not. That it was the Apostles', was never claimed by

And then the Presbyterian Church. In the Third Article of the Second Chapter of its Confession, it says: "In unity of the Godhead, there be three persons, of one substance, power, and eternity; God the Father, God the Son, and God the Holy Ghost." In its "Larger Catechism" it says more fully: "There be three persons in the Godhead, the Father, the Son, and the Holy Ghost; and these three are one true, eternal God, the same in substance, equal in power and glory, although distinguished by their personal properties."

But aside of these statements of the doctrine by leading Protestant churches amongst us, and which are

any till the time of Ambrose of Milan, in the fourth century; although substantially but in various forms, all admit its very high antiquity. That the Episcopal Church then in its first attempt at independent organization, should have retained only this Creed which, as regards the Godhead, is plainly and purely Unitarian, and not Trinitarian, is remarkable; and that in one year afterwards it should have unanimously admitted the Nicene-Constantinopolitan Creed, though by a majority it still persisted in keeping out the Athanasian, is only to be accounted for by the *in terrorem* letter of the Archbishop of Canterbury, in which he said: "Whether we can consecrate any (Bishop) or not, must yet depend on the answers we may receive to what we have written." The last Convention had repeated their request to the English hierarchy "to confer the Episcopal character on such persons as shall be chosen and recommended to them for that purpose, from the Conventions of their Church in their several States;" and for this immense boon, and to satisfy that hierarchy, through which the Apostolic succession must be had unbroken, (Heaven save the mark!) no appeal to the Gospel record, no stand on impregnable Scripture and right reason was taken; but so far, at least, submission was made before the implied if not express threat of an English Archbishop. In the same way it happened, that the obnoxious clause in the Apostles' Creed—"He descended into hell"—which on the best of grounds had been struck from the Creed by the first Convention, was restored. But how restored?

only average specimens of the statements made by all orthodox churches, how is the doctrine stated or expounded by eminent orthodox writers?

Richard Baxter, the eminent English non-conformist, says: "The Three Persons, are God understanding Himself, God understood by Himself, and God loving Himself." Doolittle, commenting on the Assembly's Catechism, says: "My admiring thoughts of God are of one single essence, yet Three in subsistence; of Three, that One cannot be the others, yet all Three are One; that are really distinct, yet really are the same." But the famous Robert South says: "There

It appears, indeed, in the body of the Creed; but a rubric is prefixed to the Creed, in which we read: "Any churches *may omit* the words, 'He descended into hell;' or may, instead of them, use the words, 'He went into the place of departed spirits,' which are considered as words of the same meaning in the Creed." This seems a good deal like child's play. The English Archbishops and Bishops in their letter, had informed their American brethren, that the article "was thought necessary to be inserted, with a view to a particular heresy, in the *very early* age of the Church." But even if so, the article is not found in the primitive or *earliest* forms of the Creed, which doubtless best expressed the faith of the *earliest* age, that nearest the Apostolic age of the Church; and the very permission to omit the article, concedes its unimportance, let it mean what it may. No unimportant article of faith should have place in any Creed, especially one to be constantly recited in public worship "by the Minister and the People." And a Creed which is professed either as Apostolic, or especially and *par excellence*, "the Apostles'," should at least have the merit of being an exact transcript of its expression in the highest Christian antiquity where it is found. I have given this matter the more space, because I take "the Apostles' Creed" so called, in its oldest form extant, to be the most Christian Creed extant; and what is even more important in this connection, utterly and emphatically anti-Trinitarian, and so far entirely unobjectionable.

is One, infinite, eternal Mind, and three *somethings* that are not distinct minds." While Bishop Sherlock says: "The Father, Son, and Holy Ghost, are as really distinct persons as Peter, James, and John—each of which is God. We must allow each person to be a God. These three infinite minds are distinguished just as three created minds are by self-consciousness. And by mutual consciousness, each person of these has the *whole* wisdom, power, and goodness of the other two."

Dr. Wallis, of the English Church, holds, that "The Father, Son, and Holy Ghost, are no more three distinct intelligent persons than the God of Abraham, of Isaac, and of Jacob, is three Gods; the three Persons are only three external relations of God to his creatures, as Creator, Redeemer, and Sanctifier." But Dr South says: "The three Persons are internal relations of the Deity to itself." Dr. Hopkins warns us that "It must be carefully observed, that when the word Person is applied to the Father, Son, and Holy Ghost, as three distinct persons, it does not import the same distinction as when applied to men." While on the other hand, Bishop Waterland calls them "proper, distinct persons, entirely equal to, and independent of, each other; yet making up one and the same being." Archbishop Secker says: "Since there is not a plurality of Gods, and yet the Son and Spirit are each of them God no less than the Father, it plainly follows, that they are in a manner, by us inconceivable, so united to Him, that these Three are One; but still in a manner equally inconceivable, so distinguished from Him, that no one of them is the other." Bishop Burnet's statement is this: "If I say the Father, Son, and Holy Spirit be three, and every one distinctly God, it is true; but if I say, they be three, and every one a distinct God, it is false. I may say, the divine persons are distinct in the divine nature; but I cannot say, the divine nature is divided into the divine persons. I may say, God the Father is one God—and the Son is God—and the Holy Ghost is God; but I cannot say, the Father is one God—the Son another God—and the Holy Ghost a third God. I may say, the Father begat another, who is God; yet I cannot say, he begat another God. And from the Father and the Son proceedeth another, who is God; yet I cannot say, from the Father and the Son proceedeth another God." Bishop Gastrell takes the ground that "The three names of God, the Father, Son, and Holy Ghost, must denote a threefold difference or distinction belonging to God, but such as is consistent with the unity and simplicity of the divine nature: for each of these includes the whole idea of God, and something more." Upon which it has been well remarked that, according to this view, "The Father includes the whole idea of God, and something more—the Son includes the whole idea of God, and something more—the Holy Ghost includes the whole idea of God, and something more; while altogether, the Father, Son, and Holy Ghost, make one entire God, and no more!" Bishop Burgess insists, that "The Father is a Person, but not a Being; the Son, a Person, but not a Being; the Holy Ghost, a Person, but not a Being. And these three non-entities (!) make one perfect Being." The celebrated Bishop Heber, one of the most brilliant members of the English hierarchy, discovered, that "The Father is the First Person in the Trinity; the Archangel Michael, the Second; and the Angel Gabriel, the Third." The learned Barrow goes a trifle more into details, and says: "There is one divine nature or essence common to the Three Persons, incomprehensibly united and ineffably distinguished; united in essential attributes—distinguished by peculiar relations; all equally infinite in every divine perfection; each different from the others in order and manner of subsistence. There is a mutual existence of one in all, and all in one; a communication, without any deprivation or domination in the communicant; an eternal generation and an eternal procession, without proper causality or dependence; a Father imparting his own—the Son receiving the Father's life—and a Spirit issuing from both, without any division or multiplication of essence. These are notions which may well puzzle our reason, in conceiving how they agree; but should not stagger our faith in asserting that they are true." And, to close my citations of statements and expositions by eminent men of this great dogma, let me place on record in these pages the words of Henry Ward Beecher: "My God? Christ Jesus is his name. All that there is of God to me is bound up in that name. A dim and shadowy effluence rises from Christ, and that I am taught to call the Father. A yet more tenuous and invisible film of thought arises, and that is the Holy Spirit. But neither are to me aught tangible, restful, accessible." While Dr. Nehemiah Adams, of Boston, says: "'Do you worship three?' is often asked. Surely we do, nor do we strive to make them appear like one. They have specific offices; we have specific wants, which lead us appropriately to worship, now one, now another, now the third."

I stop not to analyse any of these various and utterly contradictory opinions. But I ask whether the various and contradictory ways in which the doctrine is stated and expounded do not raise a strong presumption at the outset against the doctrine itself? One thing must be granted—all of them cannot be true, for they make essentially different and inconsistent doctrines. And if so, surely it is possible that even admitting the Trinity to be a Scriptural doctrine, the true, the only true, the *absolutely orthodox* mode of receiving and holding the doctrine, remains to this hour unknown, since every one of all that has been ventured may be false. Is it, then, to be believed that such a doctrine, known in reality only by its name, can be an essential, fundamental doctrine of Revelation? Would God, such a God as "the Father of our Lord Jesus Christ" is represented to be in the gospel, have left a doctrine of that character—on the belief of which it used to be said, and is even now said in some quarters, that the salvation of the soul depends—so obscurely set forth in His revealed word? Forty particulars have been noted by one writer, in which learned Trinitarians differ among themselves on this subject. I do not wonder that a mind so thoughtful, active, and free as Mr. Beecher's, should have been driven from its moorings on any of the accepted expositions of the Trinity; even though it brought up on one which, while to all intents and purposes nullifying the doctrine itself, fixes him in a form of Unitarianism of his own devising, but leaves him at direct war with the plain teachings of our Lord: or that in the distraction of thought which Trinitarian worship must, in such a mind, engender, he should prefer to worship One God, whose distinctive "name is Christ Jesus." Especially, too, if "all that there is of God to him" is really "bound up in that name"; if the tremendous alternative in his mind was—no God, except Christ be He! But I do exceedingly wonder that to one who has so diligently studied the full and blessed words of our Lord, the all-endeared, all-glorious, all-attractive Revelation of the Father which they declare, so rich in comfort, so inspiring by the light it throws on the Divine Purposes and Government, should seem to send up but "a dim and shadowy effluence"! Rob me of any thing but this great, most precious faith in an ever-present, all-gracious, personal Father in heaven! I can better afford to part with any other article of my religious belief than this of the Divine Paternity, the All-Perfect Fatherhood of God. Without it I am orphaned indeed. Providence seems an inexplicable enigma. Life a dark and stern problem. Human suffering and death stand in man's path to torture or to mock him. It is of no consequence to tell me that Mr. Beecher's Christ comprises all to him which the Father does to me. For if so, it is by exalting Christ into a place to which his fidelity and his humility alike forbade him to aspire;* the place of that Being whom, in the

* Vid. Philippians 2: 6 and John 17.—If any marvel that I cite the first of these texts here, let them remember the comment of Ambrose —"*He did not assert, or arrogate to himself, equality with God;* so that he might show us an example of humility; but *subjected himself,* that he might be exalted by the Father." The late Professor Stuart, in his

very and most solemn act of prayer, he not only addressed as "Holy Father," but testified to be "the ONLY TRUE GOD"!

But it is "a Mystery," this great doctrine of the Trinity! This is the easy and constant resort of its advocates. From the days of Tertullian, who exclaimed, "Credo quia impossibile est"—*I believe because it is impossible*—to our own, it has been their refuge, nay, even their ground of glorifying. "I ever did, and ever shall," says Bishop Beveridge, "look upon those apprehensions of God to be the truest, whereby we apprehend Him to be the most incomprehensible; and that to be the most true of God, which seems most impossible unto us. Upon this ground, therefore, it is that the mysteries of the Gospel, which I am less able to conceive, I think myself the more obliged to believe—especially this mystery of mysteries, the Trinity in Unity, and Unity in Trinity, which I am so far from being able to comprehend, or indeed to apprehend, that I cannot set myself seriously to think of it, or to screw up my thoughts a little concerning it, but I lose myself as in a trance, or ecstacy: that God the Father should be one perfect God of himself, God the Son one perfect God of himself, and God the Holy Ghost one perfect God of himself; and yet, that these three should be but one perfect God of himself, so that one should be

Letters to Dr. Channing on this passage, admits, that—"our version * * * seems to render nugatory, or at least irrelevant, a part of the Apostle's reasoning in the passage. He is enforcing the principle of Christian (Christ-like) humility upon the Philippians. * * * But how was it any proof or example of humility that *he did not think it robbery to be equal with God?*"

perfectly three, and three perfectly one; that the Father, Son, and Holy Ghost, should be Three, and yet but One—but One, and yet Three! O heart-amazing, thought-devouring, unconceivable mystery!" exclaims the good Bishop in a glow of exceeding transport, "who cannot believe it to be true of the glorious Deity?"

Here let me remark, that the fact that a doctrine is above the grasp of unaided human reason, is not alone a sufficient argument against its truth. It is not, therefore, merely that the Trinity is mysterious, that Unitarians reject it, but—leaving the purely Scriptural argument out of the question for the moment—because it is self-contradictory, opposed to all right reason, positively absurd. Trinitarians themselves have over and over again admitted this. Bishop Hurd admits that "Reason stands aghast, and Faith herself is half-confounded" at the manner in which, on the Trinitarian scheme, "the grace of God was at length manifested." South says of the Trinity in its logical results: "Were it not to be adored as a mystery, it would be exploded as a contradiction." If we are provoked to a smile at such extravagance in Protestants, who thus put themselves at the mercy of Romish critics without the slightest means of defence, we admire the bold and consistent stand which has always been taken by Romanists on church authority. It well becomes them to say, nay, to argue, and however unnecessary labor that may seem to us, set themselves to prove, as they have done, that, in the words of one of them, "the Trinity is opposed to human reason." He says expressly, "My belief in the Trinity is based on the authority of the Church; no other authority is sufficient;" and then proceeds to show that "the Athanasian Creed"—as, doubtless, the best statement of the Trinity—"and Scripture, are opposed to one another." All this is well enough—what we might expect—in a man or a church, making from the start an utter surrender of Reason before the authority of ecclesiastical tradition. Not so in a Protestant; for only by the exercise of his Reason has he become a Protestant, or can he as a Protestant maintain his position. To us a doctrine might be mysterious, and yet be entirely reasonable, and harmonize with itself. We are surrounded by, we live amidst, we constantly act upon, things mysterious. What more mysterious than God! But who of us doubts His Being and great attributes? Who does not feel, mysterious though He be, infinitely removed from our comprehension, that it is far more reasonable to "believe that He is," than to deny it; nay, that to deny it, in the midst of all this design and contrivance, this wondrous order, variety, and beauty, this fitness of means to ends, these intuitions and aspirations of the soul, would be the height of folly or stupidity? We may, we do, we often must, believe what we cannot comprehend; but never a contradiction or an absurdity.

But whence came this doctrine of the Trinity, or, in other words, what was its origin? Its origin was clearly Platonic. It was brought into the Christian Church by those of the early Fathers who admired and had adopted the philosophic views of the later

Platonists. I say advisedly, the *later* Platonists; because, in the words of Prof. Norton:* "Nothing resembling the doctrine of the Trinity is to be found in the writings of Plato himself. But there is no question that, in different forms, it was a favorite doctrine of the later Platonists, equally of those who were not Christians as of those who were." There is an obvious distinction to be borne in mind between what is positively taught by the Athenian Philosopher, and what belongs to the Platonic philosophy as held and expounded by Philo Judæus, a contemporary of our Lord, who has been styled the Jewish Plato, and by the Fathers, or Christian writers of the first four centuries. The most eminent of these men, especially those of Alexandria, the birthplace of Philo, and the scene of his labors, had in general embraced this philosophy to a greater or less extent; and they carried its modes of conception and reasoning into the faith to which they were converted. It was, as Mosheim admits, "the impure source of a great number of errors, and most preposterous opinions;" but of them all, none is more marked than this very doctrine of the Trinity, which Mosheim himself accepted. Basnage, in his History of the Jews, remarks, that these Fathers almost made Plato to have been a Christian before Christianity was introduced; in allusion to some of their efforts to show that Plato himself taught the doctrine. Cudworth, who in his "Intellectual System," has exhausted the ancient learning on this subject, says that "the generality of the Christian Fathers, before and after the Nicene

* Statement of Reasons, p. 96.

Council, represent the genuine Platonic Trinity as really the same thing with the Christian, or as approaching so near it, that they differed chiefly in circumstances, or the manner of expression;"* and declares that, "therefore does Athanasius send the Arians to school to the Platonists."† Bishop Horsley, too, in his thirteenth Letter to Dr. Priestley, says: "The advocates of the Catholic faith in modern times, have been too apt to take alarm at the charge of Platonism. I rejoice and glory in the opprobrium; I not only confess, but I maintain, not a perfect agreement, but such a similitude as speaks a common origin, and affords an argument in confirmation of the Catholic doctrine (of the Trinity), from its conformity to the most ancient and universal traditions." In one of his charges to his clergy, he says: "It must be acknowledged, that the first converts from the Platonic school took advantage of the resemblance between the Evangelic and Platonic doctrine on the subject of the Godhead, to apply the principles of their old philosophy to the explication and confirmation of the articles of their faith. They defended it by arguments drawn from Platonic principles; they even propounded it in Platonic language."

It were easy to multiply, from Trinitarian authorities, proofs which must strike every thoughtful and candid inquirer, of the Platonic origin of the doctrine under consideration. Milman, writing of "The Trinitarian controversy" at the beginning of the fourth

* Cudworth, Int. Sys., vol. ii. p. 458.

† Ib. p. 461. Ed. Lond. 1845.

century, has significant words, with which I close my remarks on this point. Having said, "This Platonism if it may be so called, was universal"—and to a degree confirmatory of the words before quoted from Prof Norton—that "It differed, indeed, widely in most systems from the original philosophy of the Athenian sage; it had acquired a more oriental and imaginative cast;" he adds: "This Platonism had gradually absorbed all the more intellectual class; it hovered over, as it were, and gathered under its wings all the religions of the world. * * * * Alexandria"—it will be remembered that this was the birth-place of the distinguished Jewish Platonist, Philo, the influence of whose writings is, as I have already hinted, so obvious on the early Fathers—"Alexandria, the fatal and prolific soil of speculative controversy, where speculative controversy was most likely to madden into furious and lasting hostility, gave birth to this new element of disunion in the Christian world."* He alludes to the great Arian Controversy, which had its germ in the anathema and expulsion from Alexandria of Arius, one of its presbyters, by Alexander, the Patriarch of that metropolitan see, for what he was pleased to style, "blasphemies against the divine Redeemer." Arius held the Father to be alone the self-existent, unoriginated God, and the Son to be "the Only-begotten, the image of the Father, the Vicegerent of the Divine Power, the intermediate Agent in all the long subsequent work of Creation." This controversy, in the judgment of the Trinitarian Milman, turned upon a

* Hist. of Christianity, Book iii. ch. iv.

"question which led to all the evils of human strife—hatred, persecution, bloodshed." "From this period we may date," he says, "the introduction of rigorous articles of belief, which required the submissive assent of the mind to every word and letter of an established creed, and which raised the slightest heresy of opinion into a more fatal offence against God, and a more odious crime in the estimation of man, than the worst moral delinquency, or the most flagrant deviation from the spirit of Christianity."

But although the doctrine of the Trinity had a Platonic origin, it is not to be understood that it assumed at once its modern form. It advanced towards that by measured steps. Previous to the Council of Nice, A.D. 325, the nearest approach to the modern doctrine of the Trinity was, that the Father alone was Supreme God, and the Son and Holy Ghost beings created by and subordinate to Him, each called God, but in a lower sense. In the Nicene Creed, so called because *voted in* by the Council above referred to—a mode of rather doubtful propriety for establishing what is Revealed Truth—"the Father" is alone described as "Almighty," and alone in the absolute sense called "One God." But "Jesus Christ" is described as "One Lord," "the only-begotten Son of God, Begotten of his Father before all worlds." Could any language more plainly mark derivation? and if in such a case derivation were rightly predicable, it of necessity made the derived being, "the Son," inferior and subordinate to the Being from whom he was derived—"the Father Almighty." "The Holy Ghost" is not even called "God" in any sense. Beyond this the church had not yet gone. The Council of Nice "established as the inviolable doctrine of the Catholic Church, that the Son is of the *same essence* with the Father; but sustains to Him the relation in which that which is begotten stands to that which begets."* It decided nothing as respects the nature of the Holy Spirit. It contented itself with simply saying, "and in One Holy Ghost." In this unsettled state the doctrine remained for more than fifty years, as we shall by and by see, before another step towards modern Trinitarianism was taken.

Before closing this Lecture, I may remark, that the word "Persons" applied to the "Sacred Three," is not in general admitted by Trinitarians to be used in its strictly etymological, just, or accustomed sense. Some, indeed, so use and understand it, and accept all the legitimate consequences; and so long as the word is used at all in connection with this subject, we have a right to hold all the advocates of the doctrine there. They are not to take shelter under any plea of mystery, where the mystery is of their own making. No word in our language has a more obvious and simple significance. The late Prof. Stuart of Andover, lamented that it should have ever crept into the symbols of the churches, and preferred "distinctions," much as Dr. South did "somethings;" while the late Pres. Dwight of Yale College, says he does not know *what* the word means, but yet thinks it "a convenient term." Convenient! for what? when confessedly it is, in the connection used, so ambiguous as to be utterly unintelligible!

* Hagenbach's Hist. of Doctrines, i. 268.

LECTURE II.

THE TRINITY—CONTINUED.

I NOW come to consider the claims of the Trinity, or the grounds on which it is held as a doctrine of Revealed Religion, and especially of the Gospel. How often and how confidently has it been called preëminently the doctrine of the Bible—alleged to be written out, nay, standing out on its pages from Genesis to Revelation in such bold relief, that "he who runs may read"! And yet nothing is farther from the truth. Beginning with the Hebrew race, in all their generations, and for whose special instruction the Old Testament was compiled, they are a standing testimony that it teaches no such doctrine. With a firmness and clearness of statement which admit of neither tampering nor evasion, they hold, and always held, that their Sacred Books declare most emphatically the doctrine of the strict, simple Unity of God. Christian Trinitarian expositors, Catholic and Protestant, affirm the same; and confess, with Bishop Burnet, "that it would not be easy to prove the Trinity from the Old Testament." Finally, the Christian Fathers did not so much as pretend that the doctrine was plainly taught in the New Testament, or by Christ and his Apostles. On the contrary, they often use the utmost ingenuity to account for the obscurity in which it was kept by them, as well as for the total ignorance concerning it of the favored people. What Christ and his Apostles did not plainly teach, would not be likely to appear in what the latter wrote. Some of the Fathers, as Athanasius, assigned as a reason why Christ did not declare his Deity to the Jews, that the world could not yet bear the doctrine; and he affirmed that the disciples had no knowledge of it before Pentecost.* Theodoret declares, that before his death, Jesus did not appear as God either to the Jews or the Apostles.† And Chrysostom not only says, that Christ did not immediately reveal his Deity, but that Mary did not herself know the secret that he was God Supreme.‡ All through the writings of these men, so far as they are preserved to us, we have their acknowledgments that even after the death of Christ his Apostles did not openly teach the doctrine; alleging the fact as a proof of their prudence and wisdom—on the one hand as regarded the Jews, who held so tenaciously the Unity of Jehovah, and whose prejudices would be shocked; on the other, the Gentiles, who might thereby be confirmed in their polytheism. Chrysostom would have us believe that the Apostle begins his Epistle to the Hebrews by declaring that "it was *God* who spake by the prophets, and not that *Christ* himself had spoken by them, because their minds were weak, and they were not able to bear the doctrine concerning Christ.§ Œcumenius, on the text in Paul's first Epistle to the Corinthians, eighth chapter and sixth verse—" There is one God the

* Serm. Maj. de fide, in Montf. Collect. Pat. vol. 2, p. 39.

† Op. ii. 15. Ed. Hal. ‡ Op. iii. 289.

§ In Hebr. i. Op. vol. x. 1756.

2*

Father, and one Lord Jesus Christ" — says: "The Apostle speaks cautiously of the Father and the Son, calling the Father One God, lest they should think there were two Gods; and the Son One Lord, lest they should think there were two Lords."* And Theophylact, on 1 Tim. 2 : 5—"For there is One God, and One Mediator between God and men, the man Christ Jesus" — says: "Because polytheism then prevailed, the Apostle did not speak plainly of the Deity of Christ, lest he should be thought to introduce many Gods." None of these writers are later than A.D. 320. Of course, if Christ be not plainly taught by the Apostles to be God, no such Trinity as is alleged can have been.

It were here pertinent to ask, what authority had these men—for whom no special illumination, not to say inspiration, can with any show of plausibility be pretended, nay, which is never assumed for them—to foist upon the Church this great "mystery," to charge upon the sacred writers this strange concealment? Every man of common-sense will answer, none whatever. The claim of such authority is preposterous, and not for a moment to be regarded. So far, however, as their admissions go to the point, that Holy Scripture, on its face and in plain language, does not teach the doctrine, the same have been made in every age since down to our own—alike by Romanist and Protestant. Learned men of the Romish Communion, though firmly holding to their Trinitarianism, make the same admissions. Sacroboscus, in his "Defence of the Council of Trent," declares that "the Arians appealed

* Op. vol. i. 492.

to the Scriptures in support of their opinions; and that they were not condemned by the Scriptures, but by Tradition." Alphonso Salmeron says: "Christ did not receive testimony from the Evangelists that he was God."* Cardinal Hosius says: "We believe the doctrine of a Triune God, because we have received it by tradition, though not mentioned at all in Scripture."† And, most distinctly and boldly, Remundus,‡ addressing the Lutherans and Calvinists, warns them in these words: "You will be obliged to confess, however unwillingly, that if you rely on the Scriptures you will be compelled to yield to the modern Arians, *no less than the Fathers were to those of ancient times;* unless, like them, you appeal to Tradition, and the unanimous consent of the Church. *They* were taught *by Tradition* that there are Three Consubstantial Persons of the same nature and essence which we worship as One God in the fulness of the Trinity; and also, that in Jesus Christ there are Two perfect substances, but only One Person. Tell me, if you listen to the Scriptures, and the express word of God alone, with what arms can you expect to engage with these men? In what way can you extricate yourselves from the *innumerable* arguments which they advance, unless you cling to Tradition, and the consent of the Church, as the only anchor of safety?" In our own day, Mr. Newman, a convert to Rome from the Church of England, in his "Arians of the Fourth Century,"* says:

* Comm. in Ev. Prolog. xxvi. tom. 1, p. 394.

† Conf. Cath. fid. Christi. cap. 27.

‡ Hist. of Rise and Progress of Heresies, Pt. i. l. 2, cap. 15.

§ Page 55.

"It may startle those who are but little acquainted with the popular writings of this day, (fourth century,) yet I believe the most accurate consideration of the subject will lead us to acquiesce in the statement as a general truth, that the doctrines in question (the Trinity, Atonement, etc.) have never been learned merely from Scripture. Surely the Sacred volume was never intended, and was not adapted, to teach our creed. * * * From the first, it has been the error of heretics to neglect the information provided for them, and to attempt for themselves a work for which they are unable —the eliciting of systematic doctrine from the scattered notices of the truth which Scripture contains."

But Trinitarians of the Protestant Faith have confessed the obscurity of the Sacred Text upon this subject. The zealous French Reformer, Jurieu,* though holding that, to deny the Trinity, was to be guilty of one of the deadliest heresies, allows, in his Pastoral Letters, that it was not known in its proper shape till the early part of the fourth century, at the Council of Nice—nay, till the Council of Constantinople—and even proves, *from the Fathers*, that during the three first centuries it was the universal opinion, that the Son was not equal to the Father, nor his existence of the same duration.

Bishop Smallridge, of the English Church, has this language*: "It must be owned that the doctrine of the Trinity, as it is proposed in our Articles, our Liturgy, our Creeds, is not in so many words taught us

* Cited in Ben Mordecai's (H'y Taylor's) Apol. i. p. 46.

† Sixty Sermons, p. 348.

in the Holy Scriptures. What we profess in our prayers we nowhere read in Scripture, that the One God, the One Lord, is not one only Person, but Three Persons in one substance. There is no such text in Scripture as this, that 'the Unity in Trinity, and the Trinity in Unity, is to be worshipped.' No one of the inspired writers hath expressly affirmed that in the Trinity none is afore or after other, none is greater or less than another, but the whole three persons are co-eternal together and co-equal." But the most striking acknowledgment upon this point from a learned Protestant, was made in a speech delivered to the Irish House of Lords by Dr. Clayton, Bishop of Clogher, on the second of February, 1756. He said: "The strongest abettors of the Nicene Creed do not so much as pretend that the doctrine of the consubstantiality of the Father and the Son is to be found in the Scriptures, but only in the writings of some of the primitive Fathers. And I beseech your Lordships to consider whether it is not absolutely contradictory to the fundamental principles on which the Reformation of the religion from Popery is built, to have any doctrine established as a rule of faith which is founded barely on Tradition, and is not plainly and clearly revealed in the Scriptures?" I cannot refrain from adding what has a strong bearing on this entire discussion, that he said: "As to the ecclesiastical history of this and the following century, (the third and fourth,) I must inform your Lordships that all those books which were published *in opposition* to the decrees of the Council of Nice have been destroyed—so that all our information comes from the other side. And of all those histories suffered to come down to our hands, I do not know of one, except Eusebius of Cesarea, (who says little on the subject,) but what is so filled with falsehood, vagaries or contradictions, that their veracity is not to be depended on."

If, then, the Trinity be not a doctrine *expressly taught* in Scripture, it can be at the best but a matter of *inference.* And so accordingly it is often declared to be by Trinitarian Protestants. The Romanist takes it on tradition, but they on inference. Mr. Carlile, in his "Jesus Christ the Great God our Saviour,"* admits that: "The doctrine of the Trinity is rather a doctrine of inference and of indirect intimation, than a doctrine directly and explicitly declared." And still further: "That a doctrine of inference ought never to be placed on a footing of equality with a doctrine of direct and explicit revelation." The celebrated Oxford Tracts ask: "Where is this solemn and comfortable mystery (of the Trinity) formally stated in Scripture as we find it in the Creeds?"† and proceed to declare it a thing of inference. The same Bishop Smallridge, from whom I just now quoted, goes on, in close connection, to say: "But although these truths are not read in Scripture, yet they may easily, regularly, and undeniably be inferred from Scripture." And well does he add: "If, indeed, it can be shown that these inferences are wrong, they may safely be rejected." Beyond all question they may; and this is the very thing I am trying to show, and hope to make plain.

The case stands simply thus: There is not a shadow

* Page 81. † Tracts for the Times, Nos. 45 and 81.

of pretence for calling it a plainly-revealed doctrine of Scripture. It is, as evidently, a doctrine of inference, and inference merely. Christ is never in Scripture styled God, identically, or, if you prefer, equally, the same being as the Father, the Infinite, the Supreme, "the Only True God." But, things are said of him, or by him, which it is supposed could have been spoken only of or by Jehovah, from which it is inferred that Christ is God. Many things are ascribed to the Holy Spirit which are supposed peculiar to Jehovah; therefore it is inferred that the Holy Spirit is God. Again: since this would look like having Three Gods, and yet God being undeniably and over and over again declared to be but ONE, it is further inferred that the Father, the Son, and the Holy Spirit, must all be that One God. And so, by heaping inference on inference, comes this Trinity in Unity. How unreasonable to call such a doctrine an essential, fundamental article of Christian Faith! The moment it is permitted to establish and require assent to one article on such grounds, where are we to stop? What might not be established in this way? By a little ingenuity, and false interpretation of Scripture language, we might infer the most absurd notions, and open a floodgate of scandal and reproach on the Truth. No; the very term *inferred*, negatives any allegation that the doctrine *inferred* is one *revealed* or *declared* to be true, and all claim to its being essential to be believed.

Holy Scripture, then, being our witness—and our appeal lies there—Holy Scripture nowhere affirms the doctrine. I say this deliberately. The direct, positive, literal, express declarations of Scripture affirm the opposite. "There is One God; and there is none other but He."* No creed in Christendom expresses the doctrine in Scripture language, for the simple reason that it is impossible. Its stoutest advocates, who most insist on calling it a plain doctrine of the Bible, who are most ready to demand faith in it as a Fundamental, have never defined, because they cannot define it, in the words of Scripture. In saying this, it is with full knowledge that our Trinitarian brethren profess to hold, nevertheless, the doctrine of the Divine Unity; nor would I cast the least doubt or imputation on their sincerity in that profession. But they hold it in such a way as seems to me virtually to deny, and practically do it away, by merging it in this great "mystery." I repeat that I do not object to the Trinity for its mere mysteriousness. As I have already said, I find mystery every where. But I do object to its unscripturalness, self-contradictoriness, absurdity, polytheistic aspect. I can see it in no other light. I can think of nothing more absurd—nothing which savors more of polytheism. That many Trinitarians conscientiously and honestly, as well as devoutly, adore the Trinity as a Divine mystery, I gladly admit; but they make or find a mystery where I do not and cannot. In me, therefore, it would be plain polytheism to worship the Three Persons each as God; and all who do so worship, are solemnly bound to see to it by their allegiance to the Truth—"the Truth as it is in Jesus"—that they have express Scripture warrant. Moreover, I say, nay, I insist, and on this am ready to join issue, that they

* Mark 12 : 32; compare 29 and 34; 1 Tim. 2 : 5 · James 2 : 19.

have no right in this or in any case to set that up as a fundamental article of Faith, to make that a condition of holding the Christian name, or of Christian fellowship, which is not taught with the utmost directness, explicitness, and perspicuity, in the Christian Scriptures. And such is not the Trinity.

Let us pass now to examine some of the arguments by which it is attempted to maintain the doctrine. We are referred to the use of the plural pronouns in the Old Testament, where God speaks of Himself, and of the plural form of the Hebrew proper names of the Deity. In the first case, only three instances occur in the whole of the Old Testament. "And God said, Let *us* make man in our image, after our likeness."* "And the Lord said, Go to, let *us* go down."† "Also I heard the voice of the Lord, saying, Whom shall I send, and who will go for *us?*"‡ Now it is an obvious answer to any argument drawn from such citations, that if these *three* seem to indicate a plurality of persons in the Godhead, the supposition is utterly rebutted by the fact, that the singular pronoun is used thousands on thousands of times, implying that God is but one Person. Besides, it is a common idiom in all languages, and in every age, for persons in authority to speak of themselves in the plural; as, for example, "We, Victoria, by the Grace of God, Queen," etc. Nothing is more common in the Old Testament. In Ezra, Artaxerxes, king of Persia, begins his royal reply, "The letter which ye sent unto *us*"—and proceeds, as if to show the idleness of the argument under consider-

* Gen. 1 : 26. † Id. 11 : 7. ‡ Isa. 6 : 8.

ation—"hath been plainly read before *me.*"* That this idiom is only a common one, and by no means indicative of any plurality of persons in the being using it, is proved conclusively in that the same Lord or Jehovah who in the second of the two passages cited from Genesis says, "Let *us* go down," says in another, with a precisely similar purpose, "*I* will go down."† In the second case, the plural forms of Hebrew names of God, the simple explanation is found in what the best Hebrew Grammars say. Wilson, in his,‡ says: "Words that express dominion, dignity, majesty, are commonly put in the plural." And Prof. Stuart, in his,‖ says even more distinctly: "For the sake of emphasis, the Hebrews commonly employed most of the words which signify Lord, God, etc., in the plural form, but with the sense of the singular. This is called the *pluralis excellentiæ.*" Learned Trinitarians, Romanists, as Bishop Tostat, Cardinal Cajetan, Bellarmine—Protestant, as Calvin, Grotius, South, Campbell, Michaelis, Rosenmüller, with a host of others, among whom are the best critics and lexicographers, alike recognize this rule of the Hebrew syntax. Trinitarians being our authority, the point is too plain to be longer dwelt upon. Not even a plurality of persons in the Godhead, much less any definite plurality such as a trinity, can be with any propriety argued from the plural form of Hebrew words.

Turning to the New Testament, the scene at the Baptism of our Lord by John is sometimes cited in proof of the Trinity, because the Sacred Three were

* 4:18. † 18, 21. ‡ P. 270. § P. 326.

obviously present together and united in one act; the Father by the voice from the opened heavens; the Son standing in the water; the Holy Spirit in the descending dove.* But surely, if any three objects could be distinct, different, apart, these were. Besides this, there are really but three passages in the New Testament, which are cited with any show of reason. The first is the Baptismal Formula at the close of Matthew's Gospel.† But nothing is there said of the oneness in any sense, of Father, Son, and Holy Ghost; no hint the remotest given that they are one. Then as to the preposition rendered *in*, it were better rendered *to* or *into;* while the words *the name of* are in the original simply an idiom of the Hebraistic Greek, in which the New Testament is written, redundant in the translation and making obscure its meaning. "Go ye, therefore," says the Saviour, "and make disciples of all nations; baptizing them *to* or *into* the Father, the Son, and the Holy Ghost." In other words, consecrating them by Baptism to the faith and worship of the Father, the Supreme and All-bountiful Source and Giver of good, spiritual and temporal; to the open acceptance and service of that Gospel of truth and salvation which He has revealed and published by His Son; and to the right improvement of those exhaustless and gracious influences by which He moves on the soul, and is ever ready to aid, guide, quicken, and strengthen in all goodness and duty. The second passage is the Benediction with which the Apostle con-

* Matt. 3:16, 17; Mark 1:10, 11; Luke 3:21, 22. † Matt. 28:19.

cludes his second epistle to the Corinthian church.* The same remark is true of this as of the previous passage, that there is no mention, no hint, of the oneness of the Father, Son, and Holy Ghost. It is simply the expression of an affectionate, devout, and earnest wish on the part of Paul, that "The Grace of our Lord Jesus Christ"—the divine favors, benefits, blessings, privileges, conferred on man through Christ and his Gospel—"the Love of God"—of that Sovereign and glorious Being, that all-gracious Father, who in His own essential and perfect nature "is Love" itself—† "and the Communion of the Holy Ghost"—the full participation of those gifts and graces, which are the earnest and seal of the Spirit of God shed abroad in the hearts of all faithful seekers—might be with all them whom he had brought into the Christian church. Where, in either of these passages, is the least trace of this amazing dogma of "Three Persons in one God"?

But the third passage to which I referred, is the famous text of the "Three Heavenly Witnesses." And in respect to this I feel bound to say, that did I not know that this text had been recently cited in a pulpit of this city, without a hint that its integrity had been even disputed, as an unquestioned and express scriptural proof of the doctrine under discussion, I should feel it labor wholly uncalled-for, and mere waste of time, to recapitulate even in the briefest manner, as I now intend, the evidence of its utter spuriousness.

Briefly, then. The verse is not found in any ancient Greek MS.; that is, in any MS. of an age prior to the

* 2 Cor. 13: 14. † 1 John 4: 8, 16.

sixth century. Bishop Marsh calls it "a passage, which no ancient Greek manuscript contains, and which no ancient Greek father ever saw."* Of one hundred and fifty MSS. of an alleged age as early as the sixteenth century, which are extant, and have been collated, and which contain the First Epistle of St. John, only two contain this verse. One of these, known as the *Codex Ravianus*, was considered by Wetstein a gross imposture; and Michaelis, who says, "it is the second of the two manuscripts which have 1 John 5 : 7," and that "it contains one half the sum total of the evidence in favor of that passage," also pronounces it "a mere imposture;" and adds: "Let it be considered in future as having no critical existence, and never quoted in support of this verse."† The other is known as the *Codex Montfortianus*. It comprises the whole New Testament, and is in the library of Trinity College, Dublin. It is really the only *genuine* manuscript which contains the verse; but it is of as recent date as the close of the fifteenth century. Bishop Marsh says that "it made its appearance about the year 1520; and, that the MS. had just been written, when it first appeared, is highly probable, because it appeared at a critical juncture, and its appearance answered a particular purpose."‡ What this "particular purpose" was, we shall presently see. Michaelis pronounces the manuscript "unimportant—on account of its modern date,"§ and says that "the *spurious* passage in the first epistle of St. John, was admitted into

* Lect. ix. † Marsh's Michaelis, vol. ii. pp. 294, 297.

‡ Marsh's Lectures, Part vi. p. 23–26.

§ Marsh's Michaelis, vol. ii. p. 284.

no manuscript before the sixteenth century.* The very tenacity with which Michaelis held the doctrine of the Trinity, made him the more desirous to keep this "spurious passage" out of the sacred text.† Speaking of the "immense weight of evidence against" it, this great critic says: "One should suppose that no critic, especially if a Protestant, would hesitate a moment to condemn as spurious, a passage, which is contained in no ancient Greek manuscript, is quoted by no Greek Father, was unknown to the Alogi in the second century, is wanting in both Syriac versions, in the Coptic, Armenian, Ethiopic, and Sclavonian versions, is contained only in the Latin, and is wanting in many manuscripts even of this version, was quoted by none of the Latin Fathers of the four first centuries, and to some of them, who lived so late as the sixth century, was either wholly unknown, or was not received as genuine."

The "particular purpose" which the "appearance" of the Montfortian MS. "answered," according to Bishop Marsh, in the extract a little above, was this: The celebrated Erasmus published his first edition of the New Testament in the original Greek, accompanied by his own Latin translation, in the year 1516, and the second in 1519. From both he omitted the verse. Assailed violently from various quarters, his answer was: "I will not undertake to add what is not in the Greek manuscripts before me." At last, however, so confident was he of his ground, he declared, that if any Greek MS. could be found which contained it, he

* Marsh's Michaelis, vol. i. p. 328.

† Id. vol. iv. 441.

would insert it in his next edition; and shortly after, the Dublin MS., before referred to, the *Codex Montfortianus*, was produced. Suspecting it all the while to be a translation from the Vulgate or Latin, as he has left on record, he nevertheless felt compelled by the word he had passed; and therefore did insert the verse in his third edition, in 1522.

In that very year Luther published the first edition of his German Bible, and omitted it. He evidently, as Michaelis thinks, must have deemed the manuscript which compelled Erasmus to insert it, "of no authority;" and nothing, either of evidence or of censure, could induce him to admit the text into any of the subsequent editions which he issued. In the last edition, which was printed while he was living, that of 1546, he made this request: "I request my friends and my foes, my masters, printers, and readers, to let this New Testament continue mine. If they find faults in it, let them make another. I know well what I make; I see also well, what others make. But this Testament shall remain Luther's German Testament. Nowadays there is neither measure nor end of mending and bettering. Let every man therefore take heed of false copies, for I know how unfaithfully and untruly others have reprinted what I have printed." Yet, strange to say, Luther had hardly been thirty years dead, before, with "Luther's Translation" on the title-page, the passage was foisted into his German text!

The verse is not in the old Latin Vulgate, or in any Latin version older than the ninth century. It is not in the old Syriac version of the third century, or in the manuscripts of the Ethiopic, nearly as ancient. It is not in the Egyptian Arabic, or indeed in any of the Arabic versions, or in the Armenian, all of the fourth century. It is not in the ancient French version, more than one thousand years old; or in the Illyrian, used in Russia, Muscovy, and by all the Slavonic races. It is rejected by the highest critical authorities of modern times, of every shade of theological opinion; besides Michaelis, as we have seen, by Wetstein, Simon, Griesbach, Le Clerc, Matthaei, Tischendorf, all Trinitarians. Bishop Lowth denies the use of his understanding to the man who would defend it. Dr. Middleton, Bishop Marsh, Archbishop Newcome, Mr. Horne, Prof. Porson, the unrivalled Greek scholar, Dr. Adam Clarke, the great Methodist commentator, abandon it. The *Eclectic Review* says: "We are unspeakably ashamed, that any modern divines should have contended for retaining a passage so indisputably spurious." The *London Quarterly*, long considered the champion of the English Established Church, reviewing Bishop Burgess' vindication of the verse, says: "The Bishop, then, on his own avowal, has been able to dismiss every doubt respecting the genuineness of a verse which is found only in a single Greek manuscript, and that of recent date; which is not quoted by a single Greek Father, nor in express terms by any Latin Father, before the sixth century; which is wanting in the more ancient manuscripts of the Vulgate or Latin; and even in those in which it is found, appears in such a variety of shapes as clearly to show, that those transcribers, who thought proper to insert the verse, had no certain reading before them. We have the most sincere respect for the Bishop of St. David's, but we cannot peruse the declaration without astonishment." * The *British Critic*, the acknowledged organ of the Establishment, reviewed, in 1830, the whole controversy, and thus closed: "Believing that the verse is unquestionably spurious, and consequently that its authenticity cannot be maintained, except by the admission of principles which would tend inevitably to destroy our confidence in the authenticity of every other passage in the New Testament, we have witnessed with uneasiness the attempt of the learned Prelate (Bishop Burgess) to establish its claim to an inspired origin, and have wondered at the arguments by which he thinks its claim is proved." To cite one more name. Dr. Davidson, Professor of Theology in the Independent College, near Manchester, England, in his Lectures, summing up the evidence on both sides, says: * "It is almost superfluous to add, that many of the most strenuous defenders of the doctrine of the Trinity have maintained the verse to be spurious; and that the great body of critics is opposed to its authenticity." Our American Prof. Stuart, of Andover, doubts, and Prof. S. H. Turner, of New-York, rejects it. All the above are Trinitarian authorities; but to any who know their reputation, quite as weighty are Unitarians like Newton, Locke, Lardner, Milton, Priestley, and our own Norton. And yet this merest interpolation, this spurious text, is still retained in our Bibles, is read in and preached from the pulpit, by men who do or should know its spuriousness, and holds its place in the Book of Common Prayer of the English Church and the

* Vol. xxvi. pp. 324 et seq.

* P. 145

Episcopal Church in these United States; where, in the Epistle for the first Sunday after Easter, it is of course read publicly once at least in the year, and probably "without note or comment," as part and parcel of the "inspired word of God"!

But admit for the sake of argument, that the verse is the genuine testimony of St. John, the Evangelist, the disciple whom Jesus loved. What then? Of what is it the proof? Of the doctrine of the Trinity? of the Trinity in Unity, and Unity in Trinity? of Three Persons in one God? By no means. Nothing of the kind. Mr. Wardlaw says: "It has been allowed by Trinitarians of the highest fame not to be so." Calvin says, that "the expression, *three are one*, must signify in agreement, and not in essence." Beza interprets it in the same way; and Macknight, paraphrasing the verse, says: "These three are one, in respect of *the unity of their testimony*." The very structure and syntax of the Greek original, demand this interpretation, and will properly bear no other.

If you will turn to the passage in our received version, you will see, I think, as corroborating the results of the best criticism upon it, that the spurious words break and mar the sense of the context. No reference, no allusion, had been made to "the Father, the Word, and the Holy Ghost," by the Apostle; but in the sixth verse he had mentioned the "water," the "blood," and "the Spirit." Hence very naturally and consecutively he proceeds, as the passage should read: "For there are three that bear record: the Spirit, and the water, and the Blood; and these three agree in one."

I return now to my main course of argument; and I say, in the first place, that the doctrine of the Trinity, if the ultimate appeal lies to the Scriptures—as with all consistent Protestant Christians it surely must—is disproved by their general tenor and drift. That is uniform to the point of the simple and strict Unity of God. Who that is familiar with the Scripture, will deny this? But in the next place, the positive, clear, unmistakable declarations of Scripture, disprove it. What can be more positive, clear, unmistakable in its import, than the language of Jehovah by Moses: "Hear, O Israel! the Lord, our God, is One Lord! And thou shalt love the Lord, thy God, with all thine heart, and with all thy soul, and with all thy might." This, too, cited and emphasized as it is by our blessed Saviour himself,* as the first and great commandment. Moreover, note the care with which the sacred writers every where distinguish and keep distinct the Father from the Son, our God from his Anointed. So remarkable is this fact, so strong and emphatic the language in which it expresses itself, that one is almost tempted to think they foresaw this great corruption of subsequent ages, and would do what they could to guard the Church against any confounding of Christ with God. For example, St. Paul says: "There is none other GOD but ONE; for though there be that are called gods, whether in heaven or in earth, (as there be gods many, and lords many;) but to us there is but One God, the Father, of whom are all things, and we in him; and One Lord Jesus Christ, by whom are all

* Deut. 6: 4; Matt. 22: 38; Mark 12: 29.

things, and we by him." So again: "One Lord, one Faith, one Baptism; ONE GOD and Father of all, who is above all, and through all, and in you all!" * In the introductory salutations of the Apostolic Epistles, mark how consistent with these statements is the language; holding this view, how naturally it expresses itself: "Grace be unto you, and peace, from God, our Father, and from the Lord Jesus Christ. Blessed be God, even the Father of our Lord Jesus Christ, the Father of mercies, and the God of all comfort." This is from the second Epistle to the Corinthians; but you will find it but an example of the uniform style of St. Paul, and with the slightest possible variation of the other Apostles. Then further; by admission of distinguished Trinitarian scholars and divines, even of Protestant communions, as we have seen, the doctrine of the Trinity is not clearly, but at the most obscurely taught in the Scriptures; is to be learned by uninitiated readers, not from the Scriptures but from the Church. The entire Romish Church takes exactly this ground, and in its extreme form; holding that though the doctrine be *in* the Scriptures, the laity cannot find it there, since it is in charge of the Church through its traditions, and to the Church must they come to learn it. Since my residence in Brooklyn, the Rev. Dr. Seabury, of New-York, one of the most learned ministers of the Episcopal Church, and at that time editing *The Churchman*, declared in its columns, that there were two rules for the guidance of Christian believers: the one, the Rule of Faith, which regarded all things *plainly*

* 1 Cor. 8: 4–6; Ephes. 4: 5, 6.

taught in Scripture, the conduct of life, and the duties of man; the other, the Rule of Tradition, which regarded things *obscurely taught* there, for example, the *Trinity*, etc. Again, the various and contradictory forms of stating and expounding the doctrine, the different senses in which it is accepted and held, raise a violent presumption against the doctrine as belonging to Christ's holy gospel; suggest and furnish reasons for the weightiest doubts of its truth; and, at the very least, stamp it as unimportant, and refute all pretension to its being fundamental and essential. Any doctrine essentially belonging to Revealed Religion, would be clearly stated in the Records of that Revelation; it would be so clearly stated there, that nobody could mistake it; it would be one and uniform in all ages of the Church, and every where in Christendom.

Here remember, that no such words or phrases as the Trinity, the Triune God, the God-man, occur in Scripture. They savor certainly far more of the subtleties of the schoolmen than of the simplicity of Holy writ. But not only are no such words and phrases to be found there, where is the known case of any man for the first time taking these Scriptures into his hands, whether in the original or in translation, in any language, in any land, with no previous knowledge of the religion they teach, with no preconceptions of Christian doctrine of any kind, and of himself finding there the dogmas which those words and phrases are made to cover? Where, in the authentic records of any Christian missionary labors, throughout the world, Papal or Protestant, is there such an experience? I confidently believe, nowhere. No such case can be cited.

No such experience is recorded or known. On the other hand we can produce two, each beyond challenge for simplicity and integrity, though very opposite in personal conditions and circumstances, of men who found in their own independent search of the Bible, the one in the original languages in which it was written, the other in a translation into his vernacular tongue, the doctrine of the strict simple Unity of God, the Father, and the subordination and inferiority therefore of our blessed Lord. I refer to the late Rajah Ram Mohun Roy, at Calcutta, and William Roberts, at Madras. The one, a high-caste Brahmin, accomplished in all the learning of the Orient; having every advantage of wealth, social position, and personal culture. The other, a native of the lowest caste, the servant of an English resident merchant, uneducated, obscure, and poor. The latter read the Bible in a translation into his own tongue, but could not find there the doctrine which the Liturgy of his master's Church, the Church of England, embodied, but only our own simple Unitarian faith. The former sought the Hebrew and Greek Scriptures, and studied them profoundly, with the same result. The Baptist Mission House at Serampore, of which Dr. Marshman was at the head, anxious to show him his mistake, detailed, as their most learned associate, the Rev. Wm. Adam, to confer with and convince the Rajah of his error, and lead him to the truth. But lo! the Rajah refuted his teacher, and converted Mr. Adam to Unitarianism; and when the Rev. Mr. Schmidt of the Baptist Mission, and Dr. Marshman, saw fit to animadvert in *The Friend of India*, of which the latter was editor, upon the first Christian publication of Ram Mohun Roy, entitled "The Precepts of Jesus," etc., being extracts from the discourses of our Lord, a discussion arose between the Rajah and Dr. M., in which the former showed himself a most skilful, able, and learned critic, and as a controversialist displayed the most generous Christian temper. His "Final Appeal" closed the controversy. Such cases, though they do not absolutely prove the truth of Unitarianism, do yet, especially in the absence of similar cases on the opposite side, increase the antecedent probability that it has a prevailing Scripture basis, and in the Christian Church has a right to be.

Where, then, do we stand? We desire, we aim to get back to the original, simple, primitive Christianity—the Christianity of Christ and his Apostles; to recover the faith which was in the beginning, long before the age of Systematic Theology. Systematic Theology—what is it the world over, but the piling up of human opinions? "Jesus," says Hagenbach, "is not the author of a *dogmatic theology*, but the 'author and finisher of our faith'; not the founder of a school, but emphatically the founder of religion and of the Church." Again he says: "The first disciples of the Lord were, like their Master, far from propounding dogmatic systems."* So Neander: "When, in the after course of development, the power of Christ's spirit, which subordinated the human element to itself, no longer predominated, but the human individuality asserted its own importance, then partial systems arose, running counter

* Hist. of Doctrines, vol. i. pp. 33, 35.

to each other, which, in one way and another, did great injury to the cause of divine truth."* Our appeal, therefore, is finally and confidently to the Scriptures. We hold no peculiar or distinguishing doctrine which cannot be stated in the express, unaltered, unqualified words of Holy writ; a thing which our Trinitarian brethren cannot do for theirs.

But we are charged with holding mere denials, with holding a purely negative faith. We answer that we do deny, in every way and form in which it is ever stated by those from whom we differ, the Trinity. We do deny that God subsists in Three Persons, in every intelligible or proper sense of that expression. We do deny the propriety of speaking of or addressing either the Son or the Holy Spirit as the Supreme God. We do deny the right, the propriety, the Gospel lawfulness of worshipping either of them as the Supreme God. In these denials we glory; because our allegiance to Scripture, our very reverence of God, our loyalty and obedience to Christ, compel us to make them. But is this all? Have we nothing but denials, negations? Far, very far from it. We affirm as distinctly, as emphatically as any, a positive, Scriptural faith. We affirm the strict, simple, undivided Unity of GOD. We affirm that He is One Person, One Being, One Conscious Intelligence. We affirm that the FATHER alone is the GOD of the New Testament. We affirm that to Him only are our prayers, supplications, confessions, adoration, thanksgivings, praises, our supreme homage and worship due. And finally, we affirm our full and un-

* Hist. of the Church, vol. i. p. 337, 6th Boston Ed.

questioning faith in the Father, in the Son, and in the Holy Ghost; we affirm it as sincerely, devoutly, heartily, gratefully, as any who bear the Christian name, and call Christ Master and Lord.

Thus denying, and thus affirming, we stand fast by our faith. Our confidence is in God, who is "able to make us stand." "To his own Master" we know and rejoice that "each standeth or falleth." While, therefore, we repudiate all that weak human presumption which might wish or attempt to rule us out of the Christian Church, "by the grace of God" our place is there, and there we mean to stay. But we rejoice that we stand, however firm and unquestioning in our own positive faith, on a broad and generous platform of hope for the world, and the largest charity. We have neither hard names nor harsh treatment for any from whom we dissent. We see alike in all, the children of One God, the Universal Father of the one great family on earth and in heaven. Differ we may, nay, differ we must, on many points from our orthodox brethren; but differ as we may, we agree, too, in far more, and those the more important ones, would they but be just and informed. We will hold our differences firmly in proportion as they seem to us important, but even then charitably. And we will pray and strive, as the great consummation, that we may thus "all come at length into the unity of the faith, and of the knowledge of the Son of God, unto a perfect man, unto the measure of the stature of the fulness of Christ."

LECTURE III

INFERIORITY AND SUBORDINATION OF THE LORD JESUS CHRIST.

MY present object, as an expounder and defender of the Unitarian faith is, to show the Inferiority and Subordination of our Lord and Saviour Jesus Christ to the Only True God the Father; in contradistinction to the popular or orthodox belief of his Supreme Deity.

On this point, as upon all points of Christian faith, the teachings of the Scriptures must be final. Whatever view of our Lord they inculcate, no other can be maintained by any Christian believer, by any Protestant at least.

A thorough investigation of this subject supposes of course that we have first the true text of the original Scripture; or second, a true or correct Translation of that text. If it be urged that such questions are beyond the reach of the mass of readers, I must admit that they are; but from that very fact springs one of the most serious and important duties of the Christian Ministry. Why set apart and prepare by long courses of profound and laborious study and mental discipline, a class of men to be devoted to that ministry, if it be not to qualify them as religious teachers as well as pastors; to interpret on their responsibility to God the Great Charter of the Christian Faith; to give the people the results of their investigations; and while, as respects every thing necessary to salvation, the simplest person may open the Bible and gain all needed light, to show that the conclusions which, by prayer and study, they have been led to adopt, are to be taken as true, and on a like responsibility received and held? Error always must be harmful and dangerous, or God would not have interposed by His revealed word. I do not say, as is often said in Christian pulpits, that unless you accept the Creed of a particular Church there is no hope of salvation for you; but I do say, that if there be error in any Creed, if it do not square throughout in every part and parcel with Holy Scripture, no matter by what human authority imposed, we are unhesitatingly bound to reject it; under the same solemn responsibility which presses upon us for the right use of every talent, opportunity, privilege which is ours; nay, more, because the interests involved are paramount to any earthly considerations.

A thorough investigation supposes, in the third place, that we arrive at a true or just interpretation of the sacred text. Such an interpretation must greatly depend upon the solution of the question, whether the words of the writer are to be taken in a literal or in a figurative sense. Undoubtedly the literal sense is in all cases to be preferred, except it violate common sense; or on its face is self-contradictory or absurd; or contradict other and plain statements or declarations of Scripture—since Scripture must be consistent and harmonious with itself. Again; obscure passages are to be explained by those which are more perspicuous, clear and explicit; so that, wherever possible, Scripture may explain itself or be its own interpreter. Still again; the great principle in this connection, the one always to be borne in mind is, that the Bible is to be interpreted as all ancient books are; that no superstitious feeling of its peculiar sanctity is to disturb or embarrass that natural course of investigation into its contents or its significance, which we should pursue in the study of any other ancient record which has come down to us. Occasional expressions are to be explained by the general, pervading sense or tenor of the book. Strict regard, as far as possible, is to be had to the time, place, circumstances of the writer, to the manners and customs of the age and country. Rhetorical, figurative, allegorical expressions or allusions, are to be specially noted, and their plain import and meaning unfolded and made clear. For example, our Lord declares of the bread at the Last Supper, "This is my body"—of the Wine, "This is my blood." Deny the principles above stated, insist on the literal meaning of Scripture being in all cases accepted, and how impregnable becomes the position of the Roman Catholic Church, including as it does to this hour the largest part of Christendom, when it plants itself on the precise words of Christ, and then demands assent to its astounding dogma of Transubstantiation!

"If," says the late Prof. Stuart of Andover, "if there be any book on earth that is addressed to the reason and common sense of mankind, the Bible is preëminently that book. What is the Bible? A revelation from God. A REVELATION! If truly so, then it is designed to be *understood;* for if it be not intelligible, it is surely no *revelation.* It is a revelation through the medium of human language; language such as men employ; such as was framed by them, and is used for their purposes. It is a revelation *by men* (as instruments) and *for men*. It is made *more humano* (after the manner of men) because that on any other ground it might as well not be made at all. If the Bible is not a book which is not intelligible in the same way as other books are, then it is difficult to see how it is a *revelation*. There are only two ways in which the Bible or any other book can be understood; the one is by miraculous illumination, in order that we may have a right view of contents which otherwise would not be intelligible; the other is, by the application of such hermeneutical (explanatory) principles as constitute a part of our rational and communicative nature." Again he says: "The Bible is to be interpreted in the same way as other books are. Why not? When the original Scriptures were first spoken or written, (for very much of them, in the Prophets for example, was *spoken* as well as written,) were they designed to be *understood* by the men who were addressed? Certainly you will not deny this. But who were these men? Were they inspired? Truly not; they were good and bad, wise and foolish, learned and ignorant; in a word, of all classes, both as to character and knowledge."*

I know how often it has been charged that Unitarians are always prompt to find interpolations, flaws, false readings, mistakes, and so forth, in the sacred text. But not more so than others who are competent to the work of criticism. All true Biblical

* Biblical Repository, vol. ii. pp. 129, 130

criticism—a science which has in our own day made such rapid progress, and constitutes so important a department of study in every theological school throughout the country and throughout Christendom; which has numbered on the lists of its devotees some of the noblest minds from century to century, in every age and branch of the church—Biblical criticism, looks to the purity of the text, before engaging in the work of *exegesis* or interpretation. Our Trinitarian brethren themselves have laid the Christian world under heavy obligations for their many examples of impartial, careful, and able critics and expositors of the sacred text; and let it be remembered that there is not a passage in the Old or the New Testament, ever cited upon any particular point in controversy between the Unitarian and Trinitarian or orthodox churches, concerning which we have not the highest Trinitarian authority for the Unitarian interpretation. We often avail ourselves of their labors gladly and gratefully. You have already observed this in my previous Lectures, and you will observe it more as I proceed. So far as the integrity of the sacred text itself is concerned, we are indeed indebted for the very best standard editions of the Greek New Testament, to the indefatigable industry and critical exactness of German Trinitarian critics like Griesbach, Lachmann, and Tischendorf. Bishop Marsh, noting the "severe" rules which Michaelis recommended for the revision and re-editing of the Greek text, says of Griesbach: "He has prescribed to himself rules equally severe; * * * * * for he has admitted critical conjecture in no instance whatsoever; and where he has expunged, corrected, or added, the evidence (which he has accurately produced) is, in point of authority, three and four-fold in his favor."* All biblical scholars at home and abroad, acknowledge that an epoch in the criticism of the text, commenced with the first publication of Griesbach's Greek Testament, in 1775–77; and now that we have the latest results of Tischendorf's and Tregelles' researches brought down almost to this very hour, we may safely say, "that the means which we have at our command for editing the Greek New Testament, very far exceed those which we possess in the case of any ancient heathen writer whose works have come down to us."† Really it seems passing strange, when we think of the services rendered to Truth, the highest Truth, by the labors of such men as I have named, that it should ever be made a cause of reproach against any class of believers, that they showed themselves anxious to have the sacred text in its utmost possible integrity, jealous for its entirest purity. Surely, if it were worthy the devotion of a life, as has been the case with so many of the classic scholars of modern Europe, to settle the true reading of some old Greek or Latin heathen writer, much more were it, when the inquiry involves the very teachings of the Anointed of God, and of the chosen and inspired heralds of his divine gospel to the world.‡

Let me in passing make another remark on what should always be borne in mind in reading and study-

* Marsh's Michaelis, vol. ii. p. 877, note 2.

† Norton's Statement of Reasons, appendix, note C. p. 440, 2d ed.

‡ Griesbach's Gr. Test was first published in this country in 1808, at Boston, from the original German edition; under the joint care of the celebrated Rev. Mr. Buckminster, and Mr. Wm. Wells, of that city; both Unitarians. They discovered and corrected several errors in the original.

ing the Scripture, whether in the original or the vernacular. The punctuation, the divisions into chapters and verses, are all modern, and of course without authority. The most ancient MSS. are with few exceptions without any points. The points at present in the New Testament are coëval with the invention of printing; and in the early printed editions varied in their placing with almost every fresh issue. The division into chapters still in use, was the work of Cardinal Hugo, who introduced it into the edition of the Bible which he published in the thirteenth century. That into verses is still more modern; and is traced to Robert Stephens, who introduced it into his edition of 1551. The titles of chapters, and running inscriptions at the top of the pages in our English Bibles are the work of King James' translators, and have nothing corresponding in the original Scriptures. Therefore, when we find printed over the first chapter of St. John's Gospel, in many editions, the words, "The Divinity and Preëxistence of Jesus Christ," we should remember that they are merely the words of the translators or editors, and no legitimate part of the Scripture; they are wholly without authority, and may be rejected by every reader. The Bible, indeed, when professedly "without note or comment," should be printed without these titles and inscriptions, since they virtually are notes or comments, and often mislead the uninstructed, who mistake them as parts of the original book. It were better also, as in some modern copies, that the Bible should be printed in paragraphs; the divisions of chapters and verses being at the most, indicated by numerals in the margin, for the sake of convenient reference. These divisions often break the connection and mar or obscure the sense. So there are many words in our English version which are printed in the *Italic* character, which is used to indicate the fact that no words answering to them exist in the Greek text; but they were inserted by the translators on their own authority alone, though in the hope, very probably, of bringing out the sense more clearly.

After these simple statements as preliminary, I proceed to the precise topic before us—the Inferiority and Subordination of our Lord Jesus Christ, as contra-distinguished from his Supreme Deity. The doctrine of the Trinity, which has already been treated, involves, and indeed declares, according to the popular theology, the Supreme Deity of Jesus Christ. Whatever force, then, belongs to the argument already urged against the one, equally makes against the other. Inasmuch, however, as we hear nowadays less of the Trinity, and more of the Deity of Christ; as, indeed, this is the great point in controversy concerning the Saviour, and is in some quarters so stated, pressed, and acted upon, as virtually to negative or destroy any proper Trinity in the sense of Three Coëqual Persons, each of whom is God, it becomes necessary very carefully to consider the topic presented.

Pray remember that I am here contending, as a Christian Unitarian, only against the dogma of Christ's *Supreme Deity*. His *Divinity* is not in controversy. The attempt is constantly made, I know, to excite odium on the one hand, or throw dust in the eyes of inquirers on the other, by alleging that Unitarians do not believe in the Divinity of the Saviour.

Nevertheless they do, as firmly and earnestly as any branch of the Church. A being may be Divine, without being the Supreme God, and such is Christ. Unitarians believe in his Divinity. They regard, honor, revere, and love him, as the Lord and Head of his Church; second only to the Supreme Jehovah in the hearts and consciences of men; the visible vicegerent and representative of the Most High.

The whole tenor and drift of Holy Scripture must leave this view profoundly impressed on the mind of any unbiassed and thoughtful reader. It every where expresses the reverse of the doctrine of Christ's Supreme Deity; every where imports his Inferiority and Subordination to God, even the Father. To this hour the existence of the Jews as a distinct people, scattered though they be among all nations of the earth, yet holding so tenaciously to the strict, simple, personal Unity of God, is a standing testimony to the fact that their sacred books, the Old Testament, contain no other or conflicting doctrine. To this day, the assertion of a plurality of persons in the Godhead, and of the Godhead or Supreme Deity of Christ, is the great stumbling-block in the way of the conversion of that people. And no wonder, when one remembers how uniform, how emphatic, are the declarations of the strict and sole Deity of their Jehovah, of His unrivalled, underived Sovereignty; the solemn manner in which those declarations were at various times promulgated, and the awful sanctions by which they were guarded. I confess my own profoundest amazement at the thought that any unprejudiced reader of the Old Testament record, should suppose for one moment that the God whom the Jews worshipped, could be any other than strictly ONE, One Person, One Being, ONE GOD.

Still, we sometimes hear it asserted—loosely enough, indeed—that "from Genesis to Revelation, the Bible teaches the Trinity and the Godhead of Christ." Aside of this language, quite too loose for serious consideration, there are some texts in the Old Testament which in the first place, it is proper to notice.

The first is Isaiah 7 : 14, cited and applied to Christ in St. Matthew's Gospel, 1 : 23: "Behold, a virgin shall conceive, and bear a son, and shall call his name Immanuel, which" (Immanuel) "being interpreted is, God with us." The whole force of the argument for our Lord's Supreme Deity, drawn or attempted to be drawn from this passage, consists in the significance of a Hebrew name, and its being applied in Matthew to Christ. But it was a common Hebrew custom to give names to children, significant or commemorative of Providential or Divine favors expected, or conferred at the time. For one example of this, you have the case of Hagar's child, whom Abram was directed by the angel to call Ishmael, which signifies, God shall hear, or God hath heard. Gen. 16 : 11. Admitting that the passage in Isaiah was strictly prophetic of our Lord, even Bishop Lowth says that in its "historical" or primary sense it referred to a child then, that is, in the prophet's time, to be born; and that before he should reach the age of knowing to refuse the evil and choose the good, that is, within a few years, (compare 8 : 4,) the enemies of Judah should be destroyed.*

* Lowth's Is. vol. ii. p. 85.

Hence that child was to be called "God with us"; God then manifesting Himself remarkably for the rescue of His people. Take, then, "the higher secondary sense" in which it is applied in Matthew to Christ, and the same meaning results. At his Advent, God was in him about to bestow the choicest spiritual blessings on mankind, to work a far higher deliverance than that of Judah. In this sense, most gratefully do all Christian Unitarians believe, that Jesus is IMMANUEL, GOD WITH US.

But, further to show the utter futility of any attempt to prove the Supreme Deity of Christ from the application of this name to him, think of the consequences to which such a mode of reasoning must lead. The argument proves, if it prove any thing, altogether too much. If the name Immanuel applied to Christ prove him to be verily God, what shall we say of the name "Abiel," which is, being interpreted, "God my Father;" or "Eli," "My God;" or "Elihu," "My God Himself;" or "Elijah," "God the Lord, or Jehovah God;" or "Ithiel," "God with me"? Well might the late Prof. Stuart admit that—"To maintain, as some have done, that the name 'Immanuel' proves the doctrine in question, (Christ's Divine nature,) is a fallacious argument. Is not Jerusalem called 'Jehovah our righteousness'? And is Jerusalem divine because such a name is given to it?"*

Again, there is the passage in Isaiah 9 : 6 : "Unto us a child is born, unto us a son is given, and the government shall be upon his shoulder; and his name shall be called Wonderful, Counsellor, The Mighty

* Letters to Channing, Miscel. p. 148.

God, The Everlasting Father, The Prince of Peace." Admitting this passage to be a prophetic description of Christ, it is obvious that the argument from it for his Supreme Deity mainly rests on the two titles—"the Mighty God" and "the Everlasting Father." That he is ' Wonderful," that he is a "Counsellor"—nay, a "Wonderful Counsellor" — as Castalio, Doederlein, Gataker, and other Trinitarians read the two words, in connection, and have high Rabbinical authority therefor—that he is "The Prince of Peace," preëminently, gloriously, no believer in Christ doubts for a moment. But what is the force of the other two phrases, or how are they applicable to him ?

As to the first, Aquila the Jew, the Seventy,* Theodotian, and Symmachus, in their ancient Greek versions of the Old Testament, and the last of them not more recent than the year 200 of our era, all omit the Hebrew word (Al) rendered in our version *God*, and read "Wonderful, Counsellor, Mighty." Le Clerc, a profound Biblical Trinitarian scholar and critic, translates the passage — "Wonderful, Divine (Al) Counsellor, Mighty." Grotius, certainly no less distinguished, also a Trinitarian—"Consulter of the Mighty God," i. e. one who, in all things, asked counsel of God. Gesenius renders the phrase, "Mighty

* The Septuagint or Seventy, is the translation into Greek of the Hebrew Bible; executed, probably, by or under direction of the Jewish Sanhedrim at Alexandria, which, in the second century before Christ, had become the residence of great numbers of that people. The Sanhedrim consisted of seventy or seventy-two members; hence the name of the Translation.

Hero."* No higher Hebraic authority can be quoted than Gesenius. In Ezekiel 31 : 11 our own translators have rendered the identical Hebrew phrase into the English "Mighty One." Prof. Noyes, of Harvard University, renders the phrase in his Translations of the Prophets, volumes which should be in the hands of every reader of the Old Testament, "Mighty Potentate," and in this substantially agrees with Luther and De Wette, and as above with Gesenius.

Here, surely, is ample authority, even the highest Trinitarian authority, for understanding the phrase in its application to Christ, in a sense far lower than that of a declaration of his Supreme Deity. Besides, Christ and his Apostles were familiar with the Jewish Scriptures, which constituted, indeed, the chief literature of the nation. They constantly quoted, and sought and used illustrations from them. Is it credible that if he or they ever supposed or understood, or much more knew, that Isaiah had in this passage foreshadowed or declared his Supreme Deity, they never should have cited or referred to the passage?

As to the second phrase — "Everlasting Father," Bishop Lowth renders it in his translation—"Father of the Everlasting Age" or dispensation, that is, the Gospel; as Bishop Jewel, in Queen Elizabeth's time says: "Esay saith that Christ should be 'Pater futuri seculi'; that is, the Father of the world to come; which is, the time of the Gospel." With this agrees Grotius; while Dr. Adam Clarke renders it exactly like Lowth. The Seventy translate it "Messenger of

* In his *Jesaia*, h. l.; as cited by Gibbs in his Hebrew Lex., under "Al;" Andover ed. 1824.

the Great Counsel" or design, and Le Clerc, "Perpetual Father;" because, he remarks, "Christ is perpetual or everlasting Father of all who shall believe in his religion." Prof. Noyes retains the rendering of our Received Version, in his note explaining the words to mean, very much like Le Clerc, "perpetual guardian and friend of his people." Any one of these various interpretations of the phrase, obviously preserves the Sovereignty and Supremacy of God, and subordinates our Lord to Him.

The entire passage, then, may thus be rendered, on the best critical authority—"Wonderful, Divine Counsellor, Mighty; Father of the Everlasting Age; Prince of Peace."

One more passage has been often cited by our Trinitarian brethren, and which I would briefly notice. It occurs in Jeremiah 23:5, 6: "Behold the days come, saith Jehovah, that I will raise unto David a righteous branch, and a king shall reign and prosper, and shall execute judgment and justice in the earth. In his days Judah shall be saved, and Israel shall dwell safely; and this is his name whereby he shall be called, Jehovah our Righteousness." Allowing, for the sake of argument, that this text refers to Christ, which is by no means clear—for Grotius thinks it rather refers to King Zerubbabel and the release of the Jews from the Babylonish Captivity—then the exposition of Prof. Noyes, in the note to his translation of the passage well expresses the prophet's meaning. "This symbolical name" ("Jehovah our Righteousness," or, as Dr. Noyes renders it, "Jehovah-is-our-salvation") "was to be given to the glorious king, the Messiah here predicted, to denote that Jehovah would bring salvation to his people by his means, or to denote what is said in the two preceding lines, that 'in his days Judah should be saved, and Israel dwell securely.' "* Dr. Ad. Clarke says: "I believe Jesus to be Jehovah; but I doubt whether this text calls him so. No doctrine so vitally important should be rested on an interpretation so dubious and unsupported by the text."† Dr. Blayney, in his note on the passage, having rendered it—"And this is his name which Jehovah shall call, Our Righteousness,"—says: "A phrase exactly the same as 'and Jehovah shall call him so'; which . . . . implies that God will make him such as he called him, that is, 'our righteousness,' or the author and means of our salvation and acceptance. . . . . I doubt not but some persons will be offended with me for depriving them, by this translation, of a favorite argument for proving the Divinity (Deity) of our Saviour from the Old Testament. But I cannot help it. I have done it with no ill design, but purely because I think, and am morally certain, that the text, as it stands, will not pro-

* Noyes' Prophets, vol. ii. p. 273. Dr. Noyes adds in his note: "In regard to the rendering *salvation*, it is a secondary signification of the original term, which, denoting *righteousness*, was used to denote the *favor* of God consequent upon it, and hence, *deliverance*, *blessings*, *salvation*. See Gesenius' Lex. That the substantive verb (is) should be supplied, is evident from the application of the name to the city of Jerusalem in ch. 33 : 16, and from the application of similar names to various persons in the Old Testament; for instance, *Elijah*. It is not at all probable that he was called *My God the Lord*, or *My God, Jehovah*, but Jehovah *is* my God. So the common version correctly renders Ezek. 48 : 35, 'The Lord *is* there.'"

† Clarke's Commentary, h. l. note.

perly admit of any other construction. The LXX. have so translated it before me, in an age when there could not possibly be any bias of prejudice either for or against the before-mentioned doctrine; a doctrine *which draws its decisive proofs from the New Testament only.*"*

It may be "a favorite argument," but surely it were a most inconclusive one. The very course of reasoning, which would from this passage prove the proper and Supreme Deity of Christ, would, from Exodus 17 : 15, prove the same of the altar which Moses built after the defeat of Amalek, or from chap. 33 : 16 of this same prophet, prove the proper and Supreme Deity of the city of Jerusalem. Precisely the same language is, in the last-named passage, applied to her.

What the "decisive proofs from the New Testament" are, we shall see by and by. What sort of proofs are devisable and relied upon from the Old Testament we have now seen. None stronger or more "decisive" than those we have examined, are cited therefrom by any class of Trinitarians to prove the doctrine of Christ's Deity.†

That Christ is *a* God in a just sense, in the sense in

* Blayney's Jerem. h. l. note.

† While these Lectures were in process of delivery, my attention was called by an anonymous note to Daniel 3 : 25, where Nebuchadnezzar said: "And the form of the fourth is like the Son of God." It is enough to say that Wintle, having rendered the passage "*a* Son of God," on the authority of Jerom and Symmachus, interprets it in his note—"Some angelic appearance." But the king himself, in verse 28, adverts again to the "appearance," and expressly calls it God's "**Angel.**"—Wintle's Daniel, p. 56, note.

which he himself (John 10 : 35) explained of others—as one "to whom the word of God came"—is beyond question. In this sense, Angels—Moses—Samuel—the Kings and Judges of Israel, are called gods. Seventeen passages at least of this character are to be found in the Old Testament.* The question, therefore, is not whether Christ is ever called in Scripture, or even whether he be, a God; but in what sense? And then, I repeat, on his own express authority in the text just cited from St. John's Gospel, he is a God as being pre-eminently one "to whom the word of God came." This was his vindication of himself when charged by the cavilling Jews around him with blasphemy, because he had, as they alleged—"being a man, made himself God." In no other sense was he a God. This, we affirm, is the obvious sense. Not that he was the Supreme God, the one Living and True God, the God over all; because Scripture forbids such a belief. To believe that, we should demand nothing less, certainly, than the clear, express, unqualified, unmistakable declarations and testimony of Holy Writ. Let us pass, then, to the New Testament.

What I said before of the entire Scripture, holds specially true of the New Testament, that its general tenor and drift are entirely adverse to the dogma of the Supreme Deity of Jesus Christ; and express his inferiority and subordination to the Father, as "the Only True God." Do you ask, what I mean by the general tenor and drift of Scripture? Precisely what is

* E. g. Ps. 8 : 5; Judges 13 : 22; Exod. 7 : 1; 1 Samuel 28 : 13, 14; Ps. 82 : 1, 6; Exod. 15 : 11, etc.

meant when the phrase is applied to any other book—namely, the first, the prevailing, the obvious impression, made by a careful perusal of the whole; as, for instance, when one reads the Æneid or the Iliad, no doubt is felt that Virgil and Homer were polytheists. So in the New Testament, the first and the most obvious impression made is, that our Lord is the Son of God, and not God himself; that God is One and Supreme; that the doctrine of its pages is consistent and uniform throughout, on this point, with that of the Old Testament. One of the scribes asked Jesus: "Which is the first commandment of all?" And he replies in the very words of Moses: "Hear, O Israel! the Lord our God is One Lord. And thou shalt love the Lord with all thy heart, and with all thy soul, and with all thy mind, and with all thy strength."* Accordingly, his constant allusions, his uniform habits of speech, his prayers, his whole deportment, are in perfect and unbroken sympathy with this idea and doctrine, nay, with this grand paramount truth. The same may be said of the Apostles.

But, more particularly; throughout the New Testament, Christ is uniformly kept distinct or distinguished from God. If distinct, then, of course, inferior—then not God Supreme. How explicit his own language! "This is Life Eternal, to know Thee, the Only True God, and Jesus Christ whom Thou hast sent."† "We

* Mark 12: 28–30.

† John 17: 3. These most explicit words of our Lord were uttered in solemn prayer to his God and our God, under circumstances and "at a moment fitted above all others for a clear and full declaration of the fundamental article of Christian belief." I quote the words of Prof. Hunt-

have peace with God," says St. Paul, "through our Lord Jesus Christ." * Two beings are here certainly brought into view. Quite as explicit as his Master's is the same Apostle's language to Timothy: † "One God, and One Mediator between God and man, the man Christ Jesus." The Apostolic benedictions at the beginning of the Epistles, are in corresponding form. "Grace to you and peace from God, our Father, and from the Lord Jesus Christ." ‡ So throughout Paul's Epistles. James begins thus: "James, a servant of God and of the Lord Jesus Christ." Peter says: "Blessed be the God and Father of our Lord Jesus Christ." § John in his second Epistle: "Grace be with you, mercy and peace, from God the Father, and from the Lord Jesus Christ, *the Son of the Father*" ‖ —he adds, as though he would have no mistake on this matter. These are examples of what is the uniform style of the Apostolic Epistles, in which in seventeen passages this distinction is most carefully observed, and in which one Being alone is always called *God*, the other, without exception, *Lord*. So in their ascriptions,

ington, at the beginning of his Sermon on the Trinity, in his recently published, and in its practical portions admirable volume, entitled "Christian Believing and Living." The words are indeed differently applied by him, but are specially pertinent to the case in hand. That sermon I have carefully studied, and cannot find in it the least strength added to the Trinitarian, or the first flaw detected in the Unitarian argument. If my readers would see the essential weakness of that sermon itself made manifest, let them turn to the masterly review of it in the *Christian Examiner* for March, 1860, and the "Two Discourses" of Rev. Thos. Starr King, delivered Jan. 7 and 14, 1860, published in pamphlet, by Crosby, Nichols & Co., Boston.

* Rom. 5: 1. † 1 Tim. 2: 5. ‡ Rom. 1: 7.
§ 1 Peter 1: 3. ‖ 2 John 5: 3.

the same is observable. Thus, St. Paul: "To God only wise, be glory, through Jesus Christ, forever."* "Giving thanks always for all things to God and the Father, in the name of our Lord Jesus Christ."† "We give thanks to God and the Father of our Lord Jesus Christ."‡ "Blessed be the God and Father of our Lord Jesus Christ."§ God is spoken of repeatedly as being "with Christ."‖ Eleven passages in St. John's Gospel alone, assert that Jesus "came from God"—"went to God."¶ Twice in his Epistles, St. Paul speaks of Christ as "the image of God."** In one he is called "the express image of God."†† In one he is said to be "in the form of God."‡‡ Whatever these passages and expressions mean, they assuredly show distinction of being.

Again; Christ is expressly declared to be inferior and subordinate to God the Father. He himself said: "My Father . . . is greater than all;"§§ and yet more precisely; "My Father is greater than I."‖‖ He is said to be "chosen," "appointed," "inspired," "sanctified," by God; "anointed," "given," ¶¶ and thirty-five times in St. John's Gospel alone, "sent" by God. It is recorded, that he came to do his Father's will—came in the name of the Lord.*** In St Mat-

* Rom. 16: 27. † Ephes. 5: 20. ‡ Col. 1: 3. § 1 Peter 1: 3.
‖ e. g. John 3: 2; Acts 10: 38. ¶ e. g. 3: 2; 8: 42; 13: 3.
** 2 Cor. 4: 4; Col. 1: 15. †† Heb. 1: 3. ‡‡ Phil. 2: 6.
§§ John 10: 29. ‖‖ John 14: 28.

¶¶ Matt. 12: 18; Luke 4; 18; John 3: 34. Any concordance will furnish the reader with references to the texts of Scripture, which are too numerous to be cited here.

*** John 4: 34; 6: 38; 12: 49; Matt. 21: 9.

thew's Gospel he is called the "Servant" of God.* Surely, the Being who is chosen, appointed, inspired, sanctified, etc., by another, must be inferior to Him. Coming, nay, sent to do His will, and receiving his commandment,† he must be subordinate to him. The epithet, servant, however "honorable," as Mr. Yates says, "on account of the majesty of the person served," nevertheless speaks for itself as expressive of the inferiority and subordination of our Lord to his God and Father, for which I contend.‡

But again; the wisdom and knowledge of Christ are declared to be derived; and if this be possible, if this be so, he must be inferior to the Source of that wisdom and knowledge, to the Being from whom he received it. "The Father loveth the Son, and showeth him all things that himself doeth; and he will show him greater works than these, that ye may marvel." "Jesus answered them and said: My doctrine is not mine, but his that sent me. If any man will do his will, he shall know of the doctrine, whether it be of God, or whether I speak of myself." "I have not spoken of myself; but the Father which sent me, he gave me a commandment, what I should say and what I should speak. . . . Whatsoever I speak therefore, even as the Father said unto me, so I speak."§ What language could be more intelligible or emphatic? How

* Matt. 12 : 18. In Acts 3 : 26; 4 : 27, 30, the word is the same in the Greek as in Matthew, and should be translated as there. Vid. Robinson's Lexicon of New Testament, p. 608.

† John 12 : 49; 14 : 31. ‡ Yates' Vind. p. 81.

§ John 5 : 19. See the whole passage to v. 30, as bearing throughout on the point at issue. Id. 8 : 16, 17; 12 : 49, 50.

impressive, in connection with the words of Isaiah!* "Who hath directed the Spirit of Jehovah, or being His counsellor, hath taught Him? With whom took He counsel, and who instructed Him, and taught Him in the path of judgment, and taught Him knowledge, and showed to Him the way of understanding?" Moreover, our Saviour admits that his knowledge was limited; and consequently, Omniscience, the knowledge of all things, knowledge without limitation, and which is an essential, necessary attribute of the Supreme God, is not predicable of, does not belong to Christ. "Of that day and hour," said he, "knoweth no man; no, not the angels which are in heaven; neither the Son; but the Father." Thus in Mark's Gospel, while Matthew reads, "but my Father only."† The Father, then, knew some things which the Son did not know. If you say, one thing, that makes no important difference. If He pleased to reserve even but one thing from his Son's knowledge, that is enough to show the inferiority, subordination, dependence of the Son. The language of our Lord is very remarkable. Had he then in his mind, all that some of his followers to this day have held and taught in mystification of himself, it could hardly have been more distinct. "No *man*" knows of it; then of course in his *human* nature—in which Christ was, both in body and soul human, a *man*, according to the popular theology—our Lord did not know of it. The "angels" do not. "The Son" does not. This title "the Son," must be taken according to the popular theology, to denote our Lord's

* 40 : 13, 14.

† Mark 13 : 32; Matt. 24 : 36.

Divine nature, his Godhead; and even in that, then, he did not know "of that day or hour." To the Father only did that knowledge belong; and hence our Lord's inferiority, subordination, dependence on the Father for all that divine knowledge he possessed.

His Power, also, was derived; and in that respect, therefore, he was subordinate to God the Father from whom he received it. 1. While he was upon earth, the witnesses of his miraculous works ascribed them to God, as his gift. After he had cured the paralytic, "the multitudes," says the Evangelist, "glorified God which had given such power unto men." * When he had called back to life the widow's son, the standers-by "glorified God," and said: "God hath visited his people." † The Apostles, after the ascension of their Lord, preaching his Gospel to Jews and Heathen, thus spoke: "Jesus of Nazareth, a man approved of God among you by miracles and wonders and signs, which God did by him, in the midst of you." "God anointed Jesus of Nazareth with the Holy Ghost and with Power; who went about doing good, and healing all that were oppressed of the devil: for God was with him." ‡ How express, too, is his own language: "All things are delivered unto me of my Father."§ "The Son can do nothing of himself . . . the Father hath given him authority . . . I can of mine own self do nothing . . . the works which the Father hath given me to finish, the same works that I do, bear witness of me, that the Father hath sent me." ‖ Then remember his words at the

* Matt. 9 : 8. † Luke 7 : 16. ‡ Acts 2 : 22; 10 : 38.
§ Matt. 11 : 27; Luke 10 : 22. ‖ John 5 : 19, 27, 30, 36.

grave of Lazarus. Martha evidently had no other ground of confidence in his power than as the gift of God. "I know," she said, "that even now, whatsoever thou wilt ask of God, God will give it thee." Our Lord seems to have "asked;" for he "lifted up his eyes and said, Father, I thank thee that thou hast heard me! And I know that thou hearest me always; but because of the people which stand by, I said it, that they may believe."—Believe—what? That I do this by my own independent power? No; but "that they may believe that Thou hast sent me." As if he had said: "For the very purpose of convincing these people of my divine mission, I thus publicly, solemnly, express my dependence on Thee for the Power, Thy Gift, which I am about to exercise."*

2. In his state of exaltation, after he had left the earth, God is still the acknowledged source of his power; while the very fact that he is or could be "exalted," implies his subordination and inferiority to the Being who did or could exalt him. After his Resurrection, and when about to ascend, to "leave the world and go to the Father," giving his parting commission to the Apostles, he said: "All power is given unto me in heaven and in earth."† He did not even then say, when his personal mission on earth in the flesh was "finished"—as though he were about to resume a place, an authority, a power which he had once abandoned—"All power in heaven and in earth is mine again;" or, "All power in heaven and in earth, which of course I could not possess in that human nature which I now

* John 11: 22, 41, 42. † Matt. 28: 18

lay aside, but in my Divine Nature ever held and still hold;" but he said: "All power in heaven and in earth" in the exalted state to which the Father now raises me, "is *given* unto me." This is the obvious significance of his words, and amply borne out by other passages. "I appoint unto you," he said to the disciples at the Last Supper, "a kingdom, as my Father hath appointed unto me."* At the effusion of the Spirit on the day of Pentecost, Peter's words were: "This Jesus hath God raised up, whereof we are witnesses. Therefore, being by the right hand of God exalted, and having received of the Father the promise of the Holy Ghost, he hath shed forth this, which ye now see and hear. . . . . Therefore, let all the house of Israel know assuredly, that God hath made that same Jesus whom ye have crucified, both Lord and Christ."† So St. Paul: "God hath highly exalted him (Jesus) and given him a name which is above every name. That at the name of Jesus every knee should bow, of things in heaven, and things in earth, and things under the earth. And that every tongue should confess that Jesus Christ is Lord, to the glory of God the Father."‡ What could be plainer, than that in his exaltation all his power is the gift of God, and held in subordination to the glory of the Father?

3. In one great province of his power, as Judge of the world, his authority and power are still conferred. "The Father hath committed all judgment unto the

* Luke 22: 29.

† Acts 2: 32, 33, 36; vid. also 3: 13; 5: 31; 1 Pet. 1: 21; Ephes. 1: 19–22; Rev. 2: 26, 27.

‡ Philip. 2: 9–11.

Son. . . . . The Father hath given him authority to execute judgment."* St. Peter declares it as the express commission of himself and his fellow-apostles, "to testify that it is he (Jesus) which was ordained of God to be the Judge of quick and dead."† This were enough. But there is a passage too remarkable to be here omitted. It occurs in St. Paul's first Epistle to the Corinthians ;‡ it forms a part of the Scripture selections in the office for the Burial of the Dead in the Book of Common Prayer of the Episcopal Church ; it probably forms part of the Burial Service as conducted by most Protestant ministers. I wonder that any Trinitarian can ever read it, or hear it read, and not feel, despite his hypothesis of the Double Nature of which I shall have more to say in a subsequent Lecture, how strikingly distinct is the Apostle's language in its expression of the subordination of the Son to the Father. "Then cometh the end, when he (Christ) shall have delivered up the kingdom to God, even the Father; when he shall have put down all rule and authority and power. For he must reign till He (i. e. God) hath put all enemies under his (i. e. Christ's) feet. The last enemy that shall be destroyed is Death. For, He hath put all things under his feet. But, when it is said all things are put under him, it is manifest that He is excepted which did put all things under him. And when all things shall be subdued unto him, then shall the Son also himself be subject unto Him that put all

* John 5 : 22, 27. But read the whole remarkable testimony to the general subject of this Lecture, contained in this entire passage from the nineteenth to the thirty-seventh verse inclusive.

† Acts 11 : 42. ‡ 15 : 24–28.

things under him, that God may be all in all." In the grand consummation of Christ's mission and office, he is to "deliver up the kingdom to God, even the Father." God (note v. 27) is to put "all things" under Christ's feet, except Himself; for the Supremacy is to remain with Him. This exception is manifest or obvious, because his own peculiar, underived "glory" He "will not give to another," not even to His dear Son.* And when "all things" are thus "put under" him by God, the Son is still to be "subject" as he always was, to the Supreme and exhaustless Source of all his power; to the God that raised him up, commissioned and sent him into the world, and who has now exalted him tc be a Prince and a Saviour.†

* Isa. 42: 8; 48: 11. † Acts 5: 31.

LECTURE IV.

INFERIORITY AND SUBORDINATION OF CHRIST. CONTINUED.

In continuing the argument for the Inferiority and Subordination of our Lord and Saviour Jesus Christ, I shall not overlook the fact, that to the force of all the language of the New Testament on which I have already commented, as distinctly teaching that fact, it is objected that, nevertheless, he is called, nay, calls himself, God, in the same sacred writings. But in passing, let me remind you that could Christ be proved to be truly God, the Trinity at any rate is not thereby proved, however many write, and speak, and preach, as though it were. The most in that case which could be made to follow, would be a *Duality* in the Godhead. Still, admitting that Christ is called, or calls himself, God, in the New Testament, the question arises, in what sense? Is it really in the sense of the Supreme, or of His Messenger and Representative?

The first proof, and one perhaps among those most frequently cited from the New Testament Scriptures, of the proper and Supreme Deity of our Saviour, is his own declaration: "I and my Father are one."* But how did he explain this declaration himself? Did

* John 10: 30.

he permit such an interpretation of his words by those whom he addressed, as is alleged? On the utterance of these words the Jews, who, I grant, seem to have understood him as meaning in the most literal sense that he was God, prepared at once to stone him as a blasphemer; and no wonder. But did our Lord admit the charge? Mark the words with which he checked their mistaken purpose: "Is it not written in your law," (a common way among the Jews of designating their Scripture,) "'I said, ye are Gods'? If he called them Gods, unto whom the word of GOD came," (i. e. who were the authorized, specially commissioned, inspired messengers of God's will, e. g. Moses, the Judges, Angels, etc., as we have before seen)—"and the Scripture cannot be broken; say ye of him, whom the Father hath sanctified, and sent into the world, Thou blasphemest! because I said"—what? that I am GOD, your Jehovah? By no means; but "because I said I am the Son of God? If I do not the works of my Father, believe me not. But if I do, though ye believe not me, believe the works; that ye may know, and believe, that the Father is in me, and I in him."*

All, then, that he admitted was, that he had declared himself to be "the Son of God"; this being, as he must have meant, equivalent to his first declaration: "I and my Father are one." The oneness with the Father which he claimed to possess, was not, then, a oneness of essence, but a oneness of purpose, consent, will, affection; such a oneness as might be supposed

* John 10: 30–38.

to exist between an affectionate and good parent and a dutiful, loving, devoted child; such a oneness, indeed, as in his remarkable prayer before the crucifixion, attesting again its subsistence between his Father and himself, he prays may also subsist among his chosen disciples, nay, among "them who should believe on him through their word" or preaching; "that they all," he says, "may be one; as Thou, Father, art in me, and I in Thee, that they also may be one in us."* St. Paul spoke of Apollos and himself as One, in the same sense;† such phraseology is very common in Scripture.

But the advocates of the doctrine of the proper Deity of our Lord, often insist that the title, "Son of God," proves it. The title, "*Son of God*," is given to Christ some fifty times, and "*the Son*," some forty times, in the New Testament. How strange that either should be thought to prove so stupendous a doctrine, as that he is the Supreme God! The term *Son*, certainly in every other case that can be named, implies distinction from, subordination to, another, a Parent; why not here? Is it urged that, at any rate, it shows his Divine nature? In general terms that may be granted; but not that he is the same person or being—not surely the Supreme God. Angels, Israelites, Solomon, Christians, repeatedly are all called sons of God in the Old and New Testaments.‡ Applied to Christ, it is an eminently glorious title, expressive of God's spe-

* John 17. † 1 Cor. 3 : 6, 8.

‡ Job 1 : 6; 38 : 7; Hosea 1 : 10; 2 Sam. 7 : 14; Rom. 8 : 14 1 John 3 : 1; Gal. 4 : 4–7; John 3 : 12.

cial love, approval, etc., and of his own intimate connection with God—yet not less of his personal dependence and consequent subordination and inferiority. Sixty-six times God is expressly called *his* Father; repeatedly, *his* God; interchangeably and equally, "*his* God and our God, *his* Father and our Father." Even after his Resurrection, he said to Mary: "Go to my brethren, and say unto them, I ascend unto my Father and your Father; and to my God and your God."* What must she, what must they, have understood by such a plain and distinct declaration? What reason did he ever afterwards, did he ever before, give them for interpreting it otherwise than according to its simple, obvious meaning?

Again: we are referred to the words of Thomas, after the Resurrection, who, on being convinced of that stupendous fact by our Lord's offering him the very evidence he demanded, exclaimed: "My Lord and my God!"† But if Thomas did thus really acknowledge his Master to be God, I should still insist that it was only in the sense of one "to whom the word of God came." Thomas, as a devout Jew, well knew that "no man hath seen God at any time"; his Master he had seen frequently, times without number. Our Lord had said to the woman of Samaria, "God is a Spirit"; and in perfect correspondence with that declaration, when he perceived the fright into which his disciples were thrown at his first appearance among them when "gathered together," he said: "A spirit hath not flesh and bones, as ye see me have."‡ Surely

* John 20 : 17. † John 20 : 28. ‡ Luke 24 : 39.

it is nothing but absurd to suppose that Thomas believed the being before him, who gave to him sensible demonstration that he had "flesh and bones," was the *Invisible* God, as the sacred writers so often style the Almighty.* Under the circumstances, the words seem to me only a perfectly natural expression of sudden and intense surprise and astonishment—the language of strong emotion on the part of Thomas. Of what was the disciple incredulous? Simply of the fact of his Lord's being alive again, the fact of his Resurrection. At what was he surprised? That there was given him the identical evidence, without which he had declared he would not believe that the others had "seen the Lord"—that he was alive again—that he had come forth from the dead. "A spirit"—an apparition—a phantasm that "had not flesh and bones"—they might have seen; but not Jesus, their beloved Master; not him, again in the flesh. That was the point to be proved, and nothing else, nothing more. Nothing as to his nature, rank in creation, or indeed, what or who he was. But simply and only the actuality of the Lord's Resurrection, his personal identity with the crucified and buried Christ. What wonder at the astonishment or even awe which filled Thomas, when the proof he needed and asked was vouchsafed, and he felt that his revered, beloved, divine Master, stood before him! What wonder that he, an Oriental—"according to the invariable habit of the Jews, Arabs, and almost all other Asiatic nations, who, when struck with wonder, often make exclamations in the name of the

* Col. 1:15; 1 Tim. 1:17; Heb. 11:27

Deity"*—thus surprised and struck with this marvellous, this astounding fact, should have exclaimed in the fulness of his emotion, "My Lord and my God!" The language of mere confession—when he would have said, "*Thou art* my Lord; *thou art* my God"—was too cold for the state of mind in which Thomas was. Our Lord understood that state of mind in his incredulous follower, and his response to the exclamation shows it: "Because thou hast *seen*"—because thou hast seen that it is a being having flesh and bones—"thou hast believed" that it is really I, risen from the dead, and not a mere apparition; "blessed are they that have not seen and yet believed!"

There is a very acute remark of Prof. Norton, well worthy of attention in this connection. "Supposing that Thomas *had* believed, and asserted that his Master was God Himself; in what way should this affect our faith? We should still know the fact on which his belief was founded, the fact of the Resurrection of his Master, and could draw our own inferences from it, and judge whether his were well-founded. Considering into how great an error he had fallen in his previous obstinate incredulity, there would be but little reason for relying upon his opinion as infallible in the case supposed. I make this remark, not from any doubt about the meaning of his words, but, as I have said, for the purpose of pointing out one example of that incomplete and unsatisfactory mode of reasoning, which appears in the use of many quotations from the Old and the New Testaments."†

* Ram Mohun Roy's Final Appeal, p. 232.

† Norton's Statement of Reasons, 2d ed. pp. 302, 303.

Well may we say, with the Roman Catholic Salmeron, that "Christ did not receive testimony *from the Evangelists*, that he was God."* The Gospels, of which they were the writers, give no such testimony. In making this assertion, we have more than Roman Catholic admissions, however, to sustain us. Protestant Trinitarian divines have repeatedly made the same. Many, with Dr. Longley, Bishop of Ripon, have been forced to account in the best way they could, for the obvious and remarkable silence or reserve of the Evangelists, on so fundamental a point of Christian faith as they affirm this to be; and like him have held that before the descent of the Holy Ghost at Pentecost, they were designedly kept in ignorance of it by our Lord himself, as not being till then "able to bear" so startling a disclosure.† To such shifts are the advocates of the Supreme Deity of Christ driven, by the difficulty of reconciling it with the whole tenor and drift of the Gospel histories. But what if it were so? What if they did not know that their Master was God, till they had shared the special illumination of Pentecost, or that which immediately followed? They assuredly, according to all critical authority, did not write their Gospels till long after this. The earliest date assigned to either of the Greek Gospels is A.D. 60. Is the marvel of the absence of the least hint or trace of any such doctrine, or of their singular reserve upon it, throughout the four, materially lessened by the supposition referred to? *They* knew it all the while. To them it

* Comm. in Evang. tom. i. p. 394.

† Vid. the Bishop's "Brothers' Controversy," pp. 54 et seq.

must have been, whenever communicated, most amazing, that he with whom they represent themselves to have *made so free* — conversing unembarrassed with him, catechising him, contradicting him, rebuking him, and finally deserting and denying him when arrested, put through a mock trial, condemned, and crucified, was, nevertheless, their GOD! Yes, all the while they were writing their memoirs of him, they knew this, and yet, without one word of comment, record his words: "I can of mine own self do nothing" —"My Father is greater than I"—"I came not to do mine own will, but the will of Him that sent me"! On far less important points they thought it worth while to throw in a word of explanation;* but on this, not one. Is it credible, that with their minds possessed of this grand, yet overwhelming idea of their Master, nay, knowing verily, beyond question, by direct revelation, that he was God, they could thus calmly, with no emotions of awe which we can discover, write out their several accounts of him in such a way, that had these Gospels perished, and no other books been written by his followers, the world would have been in the dark to this hour on this momentous subject? Nay, more; take the case of John the Beloved, the last of the Evangelists, who wrote his Gospel in his old age. Is it credible that he, near the close of that Gospel, knowing at that moment as is generally understood, all that the other three gospels contained or omitted, and having brought his own narrative down to the Resurrection of his Master—knowing at the

* E. g. John 12 : 33; 21 : 19.

same time that that Master was God, very and Supreme God—should nevertheless have thus summed up, and declared the great and special purpose of his work? "These are written, that ye might believe that Jesus is"—what, or who, I ask? God? No—nothing like it. A clear, broad line of separation is preserved, perfectly corresponding to all that he and the other Evangelists had before recorded, perfectly in accordance with the whole tenor and drift of the entire New Testament. "These are written, that ye might believe that Jesus is the CHRIST, the SON of GOD; and that, believing, ye might have Life through his name." Even Dr. J. Pye Smith says:* "It is plain that the immediate object, in the writings of Matthew, Mark, and Luke, was to produce a conviction that Jesus of Nazareth was *the Messiah* announced and described in the prophetic writings." Yes, and the same was John's, as the passage just quoted from his Gospel shows. He had written all he had written there; all, including every text and passage ever since cited to prove either a Trinity of Persons in the Godhead or the Godhead of Christ—he had written it all to convince his readers, to make them "believe" just this one great, fundamental truth, namely, "that Jesus is the Christ," i. e. the Messiah, the two terms meaning precisely the same; the latter from the Hebrew, the former from the Greek: that he is "the *Son* of God" and not God Himself. Nay, more; to show that this was the essential thing to be believed, he adds: "And that believing, ye might have Life through his name."† "Life"

* Scrip. Test. to the Messiah, vol. ii. p. 412.

† John 20: 31.

here includes all, in the highest sense, which our Lord promises to his faithful followers; and all the knowledge of his Master necessary to secure to us that, John has unfolded in his precious pages. It is, I repeat, "that Jesus is the Christ, the Son of God."

But there is an equal silence and reserve in the Acts of the Apostles, which book tells us of the wonderful doings at Pentecost; and in the several Epistles and the Revelation. The dates assigned to all these books are long after Pentecost, although some of the Pauline Epistles are earlier by a few years than the Gospels; and still not a trace of the Godhead of Christ is in any of them. I do not say that they furnish those who differ from us no *alleged* proofs of the doctrine, for these alleged proofs are what we are now to sift. To them let us proceed.

In the Acts* we read of "the church of God which he hath purchased by his own blood." I might remark upon the strangeness of such language, having no parallel to it throughout the Scriptures, and at first sight, and even the more we reflect on and analyse it, shocking to every unsophisticated mind. The "blood" of God! But we need not spend much time about it, for Griesbach, after most careful examination of manuscripts, Wetstein, Le Clerc, and Grotius, all read "church of the Lord." Adam Clark, in his notes on the passage, though admitting this reading to have "the greater evidence," thinks it necessary to add, "We must maintain that, had not this Lord been God, his blood could have been no purchase for the souls of a lost world"; so, according to him, it might as well

* 20 : 28.

read, after all, as in our English version. But Kuinoel, Bishop Middleton, Dr. J. P. Smith, Bishop Marsh, and Olshausen, (whose great Commentary has been recently translated by Dr. Kenrick, of Rochester University,) are explicit in favor of Griesbach's reading; "which," says Olshausen, "*all* recent critics recognize as the right one."* Prof. Stuart, and Dr. Barnes of Philadelphia, are of the same mind; and nothing more need be said of a text, which is thus relieved of all difficulty, and furnishes not a shadow of support to the doctrine I am controverting.

In the Epistle to the Romans,† we read: "Christ . . . . who is over all, God blessed forever. Amen." But look at the passage. He is recounting the distinctive and glorious privileges of the Jews; and, in the third verse, so profound is his interest and anxiety for their salvation, that he almost wishes himself "accursed," or, as the margin reads, "separated from" Christ, for their sake. What is his object? To vindicate the call of the Gentiles into, and the rejection of the Jews as such, from the Christian Church. Throughout the Epistle he seeks to meet and neutralize Jewish prejudices, and the opposition of his "brethren," his "kinsmen according to the flesh," to the new faith. Would he have been so infatuated as the Trinitarian construction of this text would make him? When he knew how tenaciously, not to say bigotedly, the nation clung to the Unity of GOD, would he, having in mind the obvious pupose stated above, have riveted at the start all their prejudices, and confirmed

* Kenrick's Olshausen, vol. iii. 384. † 9: 5.

all their opposition, by asserting that that Jesus whom they had crucified as a malefactor, was nevertheless that God Himself? Besides, how abruptly, without cause or connection, is such a tremendous statement as is supposed, here introduced! No use appears for it, or is made of it by St. Paul. Nowhere else does he, or any of the sacred writers, call Christ "God over all, blessed forever." Directly the contrary, as we have already seen, and shall see again. Remember, moreover, that the punctuation of the text is a modern and purely arbitrary matter. Every scholar knows that it must depend on what the reader understands this or indeed any passage to mean; for the Apostolic autographs were probably without any punctuation, as are the most ancient manuscripts. Accordingly, we find critics and versions differ, and often widely, in their pointing of this and of other texts. Lachmann, Tischendorf, Rückert, and a host of the ablest critics, put a period after the word *flesh*, and read: "Of whom Christ came, according to the flesh. He, who is above all God, be blessed forever!" or, "God, who is above all, be blessed forever!" Erasmus, without positively adopting it, declares that this punctuation "is perfectly suitable to the purport of the discourse." It is also remarkable, that though the ancient Greek manuscripts are in general without punctuation marks, the celebrated *Codex Ephraemi*, one of the most authoritative among them, has actually, as above, a period after the word "flesh." With this construction, the clause under consideration becomes a Doxology, or ascription of praise to God for the coming of His Christ or Messiah, in the prophetic line of "the covenants . . . the promises . . . the fathers;" His preëminent gift. As such, it must be presumed, according to the uniform style and custom of St. Paul,* to have been addressed to the Father as "God above all," and not to Christ.

Besides, the Apostle had just before (v. 3) spoken of himself in reference to his human lineage, in the exact phrase in which he now speaks of Christ—"according to the flesh"—referring to his own earthly descent. Would he immediately, on the instant, have declared him, nevertheless, with no explanation, with no connecting clause, and for no conceivable purpose, to be the self-existing, Supreme God? Would this, I again ask, have been in the least likely to conciliate the Jews? No, no. Depend upon it Paul was too sagacious, too acute, too logical, at the outset of his argument to proclaim, even if in the sequel he meant to prove, that the Crucified was their GOD.

And the History of the Church sustains our interpretation of the text. For why, during that whole Arian controversy which raged so fiercely and lasted so long, was this text never once quoted against the Arians, if it so clearly attested the Supreme Deity of Christ? "Those," said Erasmus, "who contend that in this text Christ is clearly called God, either place little confidence in other passages of Scripture—deny all understanding to the Arians—or pay scarcely any attention to the style of the Apostle. A similar passage occurs in 2 Cor. 11:31: 'The God and Father of our Lord Jesus Christ, *who is blessed for ever;*' the latter clause being undeniably restricted to the Father."†

* Vid. Rom. 1 : 25; 2 Cor. 1 : 3; id. 11 : 31; Eph. 1 : 3.

† Erasmus Annot. in op. tom. vi. p. 611.

I pass now to another passage, from St. Paul's first Epistle to Timothy;* where, it is alleged, that the Apostle speaks of Christ as "God . . . . manifest in the flesh." I might occupy much time in citations from various critics upon the true reading of this passage in the Greek. Suffice to say that many, very many of the most repute reject the word answering to *God*, and substitute the pronoun answering to "who" or "he who"; Griesbach, Wetstein, Lachmann, De Wette, do this. Bishop Marsh says that "this reading (God) is found *a prima manu*† in not a single ancient manuscript in uncial letters, (or capitals—the highest class of MSS.) nor in a single ancient version, except the Arabic, which is of very little authority." Prof. Stuart, of our own country, who holds to the reading of our English version, nevertheless says, that an attentive student of Scripture, "will see that God might be manifest in the person of Christ, without the necessary implication of the proper divinity (Deity) of the Saviour."‡ Here I leave the critics. I take the common reading. The Unitarian gladly believes that God did manifest himself in Christ preëminently. He can as consistently and sincerely speak of Christ as "God manifest in the flesh," as any other Christian of any other name. Yes, I accept the statement to the full. I rejoice and bless God who has been pleased thus gloriously and graciously to manifest Himself in the person of His beloved Son our Lord. In him God comes near to man. His power and wisdom, his

* 1 Tim. 3:16.

† *At first hand*, i. e. in the original transcript.

‡ He refers to John 17: 20–26; 1 John 1: 3; 2: 5; 4: 15, 16.

"grace and truth," what were they all but God's? So high do I place him in my devout contemplation and faith, that what he taught, commanded, threatened, or promised, has with me all the weight and authority which could belong to the same words were they audibly addressed to me by God himself from the opened heavens. He is simply Inferior and Subordinate to God, because, from the necessity of the case, the Supreme can have no Equal.

LECTURE V.

INFERIORITY AND SUBORDINATION OF CHRIST CONCLUDED.

THERE remain some other passages of the New Testament Scripture to be examined before leaving the topic of the Inferiority and Subordination of our Lord Jesus Christ. In the Epistle to the Hebrews* we read, "But unto the Son he saith, Thy throne, O God, is for ever and ever;" and therefore it is alleged that this proves the proper Deity of the Son. One would think it were only necessary to read the context to see that it proves no such thing, but only that the Son is addressed as God in the lower sense in which they were so addressed "to whom the word of God came." Mark the language. "Thy throne, O God, is for ever and ever. . . . . Thou hast loved righteousness and hated iniquity; *therefore* GOD, even *thy* GOD, hath anointed thee with the oil of gladness *above thy fellows.*" Whatever rank or office the title *God*, in the first instance, implied, it was plainly subordinate to that of the Supreme. He to whom it is applied has himself a Superior, nay, a GOD—which could not be said of the Supreme; is rewarded for his fidelity, his love of righteousness — being "*therefore* anointed," etc. — (but

* 1 : 8.

who could "reward" the Supreme?); has "fellows," equals—which it were simply absurd to predicate of the Supreme. The passage is a quotation from one of the Messianic Psalms, or those which the Jews believed to be prophetic of their king Messiah;* and nothing is more beyond dispute than that the Jews expected in their Messiah, although a King, a mighty leader, deliverer, conqueror; still, only "a man born of human parents;"† with which ideas, assuredly, the entire passage is simply consistent.

When we turn to the critics, even prominent Trinitarian critics, our view of the passage is confirmed. Grotius, and many others before and since the time of Griesbach, read the passage conformably to the text of the latter, "God is thy throne" in the first clause. So Calvin, so Nösselt. Dr. Mayer, in the Biblical Repository,‡ says: "Here the Son is addressed by the title *God;* but the context shows that it is an official title, which designates him as a King; he has a kingdom, a throne, a sceptre; and in verse 9 he is compared with other kings, who are called his fellows; but God can have no fellows." Prof. Stuart, in his Commentary on the Epistle, says: "That the whole Psalm relates to the Messiah as *Mediatorial King*, can scarcely be doubted by any one who compares together all its different parts." And although he had, "in a former publication," contended that the title *God*, by which he (the Son) is here addressed, denoted his

* Ps. 45: 6, 7.

† Vid. Just. Martyr's "Dial. cum Trypho," p. 235, *et alibi*, cited by Prof. Norton. "Reasons," etc. pp. 204–5.

‡ January, 1840, p. 149.

"divine nature," he finds grounds to doubt. In the Biblical Repository,* however, his doubt is resolved, for there he says: "As to the quotation from Ps. 45, it seems to me a clear case, that it does not fairly establish the truly divine nature of him to whom it is applied."

I pass to another passage in the first Epistle of John:† "We know that the Son of God is come, and hath given us an understanding, that we may know Him that is true: and we are in Him that is true, *even* in His Son Jesus Christ. This is the true God, and eternal life. Little children, keep yourselves from idols." In the first place, the Trinitarian mistake upon this passage is perpetuated without just reason, from the introduction most improperly of the word "even" into the text, there being no word in the original answering to it, as is shown by the use of the italic type. In the next place, the chief difficulty arises from the pronoun rendered "This" often made to refer to the nearest antecedent or "Jesus Christ." But Grotius says: "The pronoun *this* not unfrequently relates to a remote antecedent, as in Acts 7 : 19, (where it is rendered 'the same';) id. 10 : 6," (where it is rendered "he" ‡;) and Vater: "There is no reason why the words *this is the true God* should not be referred to the same, (*Him that is true*,) though grammatically they belong to the proximate antecedent *Christ*." Both these are Trinitarian authorities; but I cannot omit citing

* No. for July, 1835, pp. 105, 106. Comm. in Hebr.; p. 294, 2d ed.;—the whole note is remarkable for its candor.

† 4: 20, 21.

‡ Another example of reference to *the remote antecedent* occurs in Act. 4: 11; and a very remarkable one in 2d Ep. of John, ver. 7.

from another of the same class more at length. Lücke, in his comment on the passage,* says: "1. The emphatic tone of the preposition renders it necessary to refer '*this*' to the prevailing chief subject of the preceding preposition. But this is God, '*Him that is true*,' and not Christ, who only is mentioned parenthetically, as he through whose mediation the *being in Him that is true* is effected. 2. Further, as God above is *by excellence*, and without any word additional, called 'The True,' (compare John 17 : 3,†) and Christ never is so styled by St. John; '*this*' can, according to all rules of logical interpretation, not be referred to Christ, but to God, unless we are determined to charge St. John with an intentional confusion of ideas. 3. The authors of the New Testament never use the same predicate and name for the Father and the Son of God, when they speak of each distinctly. Here it is plain that they are distinctly spoken of. If, then, '*this*' here ought to be referred to Christ, we should have a confusion of names and predicates, to which there would be no parallel in the New Testament. Finally, 4. St. John indeed calls the *Logos of God* in Christ, God, in John 1 : 1; but the historical Christ he never does so designate, but always as *Son of God*. But let us suppose that St. John intended to designate Christ as *the True God*, for what reason does he introduce that designation in this particular place? Are we to suppose that without demonstration, without preparation of any kind, nay, even

* Lücke's Comm. on St. John's Epistles, in h. l. Edinburgh ed. 1837.

† "This is life eternal, to know Thee, *the only True God*," etc.

contrary to the nearest context, he introduced such an important, and with him unusual proposition," (I beg my readers to note the strength of these expressions by a Trinitarian writer,) "in such an equivocal form as a straggler at the end of the epistle—that he did so introduce a proposition, to which nothing resembling it occurs in the whole epistle, and to which no satisfactory clue is to be found in the Gospel which mentions as God only the *Logos* or *Word* in Christ—always speaks of the Christ who appeared in the flesh as *Son of God*—and says of the Father of Jesus Christ, John 17 : 3, that He is 'the Only True God'? Never! And the warning against idols, plain and well grounded as it appears, if '*this*' is referred to God, how obscure and unconnected, nay, how confused must it appear to the reader when, besides God, Christ also is mentioned as *the True God!* These are sufficient grounds for declaring, that the only right construction is to refer '*This is the True God*' to God."

With such ample support from men eminent in the Trinitarian ranks, not to cite from Erasmus, Wetstein, Michaelis, Archbishop Newcome, Neander, and many others, to the same effect, there can be little difficulty in understanding the text. Newcome says, in his notes upon it in his translation: "*He that is true* must be different from the person who gave man an understanding to know him." And he thus translates it—"that we may know Him that is true: and we are in Him that is true, through His Son Jesus Christ;"—that is, as he says again—"by means of, by the manifestation of, his Son Jesus Christ. This rendering occurs in our old English Bibles;" and he refers to the editions of 1549,

'51, and '68. Still farther, in a note on the last clause of verse 20, he thus expounds it: "By Him that is true, I mean the true God, and the Giver of everlasting life." With Newcome, substantially, agrees Prof. Norton, who thus translates: "And we are assured that the Son of God has come, and has given us understanding to know Him who is True, and we are with Him who is True, through His Son Jesus Christ. He is the true God, and eternal life. Children, keep yourselves from idols." He adds: "The meaning is, that He with whom Christians are, He who is True, is the True God, and the Giver of Eternal Life. In the former part of the passage, St. John expresses the Jewish conception of the personality and power of Satan. To him, the wicked one, he regarded the heathen world as subject; while believers were through Christ with Him who is True, the True God. They were, therefore, to keep themselves from idols."*

There is another text in this Epistle:† "Hereby perceive we the love *of God*, because he laid down his life for us." It is enough to say of this that the words "of God"—italicised, remember, by our own translators as not in the Greek, are absolutely rejected by Wetstein, Griesbach, Mill, Bengel, and a host of other distinguished critics. The reference is unquestionably to Christ.

Then as to the declaration of our Lord, recorded in the *Gospel* of St. John:‡ "Before Abraham was, I am." Why, it may be asked in the outset, why, ex-

* Norton's Reasons, etc. pp. 197–8.

† 1 John 3 : 16.

‡ John 8 : 58.

cept for a purpose, have our translators departed here from their usual mode of rendering the exact Greek word so often used by our Lord? Here it reads, "I am"—literally, and without supplement; in other places, "I am *he*"?* Why not here as there—"I am *he*"—the Messiah purposed in the counsels of God long before Abraham had being? This is the interpretation of Grotius, and I believe the true one. Trinitarians are accustomed to insist that our Lord meant to declare that he was the "I AM" of the Old Dispensation, who revealed Himself to Moses by the name or appellation, "I am that I am"; but Dr J. Pye Smith tells us† that "the words" there "are in the future tense, 'I will be that which I will be,' Exod. 3 : 14; and most probably it was not intended as a name, but as a declaration of a certain fulfilment of all the promises of God." While Mr. Carlile of the Scotch Kirk says:‡ "I do not mean to rest any argument on the expression *I am*, taken by itself. It occurs repeatedly in this chapter, and is translated *I am he.*"

If then the use of the word was no assumption, as of inherent right by our Lord, of the alleged name or appellation of Jehovah, the rendering of the Common Version is meaningless. What our Lord meant was, that before Abraham was born, God had purposed that he should be the Messiah. So to speak, in allusion to the Divine purposes, was familiar to the Jews. In Jer-

* Vid. in this same chapter, vv. 24, 28; also, John 4 : 26; 13 : 19. Compare also Matt. 24 : 5; Mark 13 : 6, and Luke 21 : 8; also, John 3 : 28 and Acts 13 : 25.

† Scripture Test. vol. ii. p. 161.

‡ "Jesus Christ the Great God our Saviour." p. 174.

emiah,* God says to the prophet: "Before I formed thee in the womb I knew thee; before thou camest forth at birth I sanctified thee; and I ordained thee a prophet unto the nations." Repeatedly in this very chapter he had used the same phrase, "I am;" and as repeatedly our translators render it, as essential to the sense, "I am *he*," that is, the Messiah, for whom the Jews had been long looking. That was what they, he had said must believe, or "die in their sins"; that was, as he had just before told them, what they would "know" when they had "lifted him up"; and that was what he now declared himself to have been in the omniscient counsels of God, long before the era of the great Patriarch.†

Again we are referred to the following passage in proof of the proper Deity of our Lord. "Who, being in the form of God, thought it not robbery to be equal with God."‡ Assuredly the Trinitarian exposition of this text, is a mere *reductio ad absurdum* of the Apostle's argument, since it makes him say that Christ, being God, thought it no robbery to be equal with himself! It would indeed be absurd to say that of any thinking being. St. Paul would hold up to the imitation and admiration of the church at Philippi, our Lord's example of humility and obedience. "Be the same mind in you," he says, "which was also in Christ Jesus; who, being as God, inasmuch as he was the brightest manifestation of God, His chosen messenger and Representative, the 'beloved Son,' the 'only-begotten of the Father,' did not think this glorious similitude a

* Jer. 1. † Verses 24, 28, 58 ‡ Philippians 2 : 6.

thing eagerly to be clung to or retained; but rather laid it aside, became a servant, assumed the condition of a man; and being in that condition, humbled himself and was obedient even unto death, the death of the cross." Such I take to be the Apostle's meaning, according to the idiom of our own language. And the whole life and history of our Lord well warrant what he says. Speaking the words of God—wielding miraculous power by His Gift, and thus doing the works of God—possessed of Divine wisdom and authority by the will of the Father, he did not eagerly grasp at the grandeur of his high office, or hold or use its great powers for personal advantage; but in the condition of an humble and faithful servant, labored on in poverty and contempt for the good of others;—in that of a man, though despised, rejected, reviled, insulted, persecuted, hunted down even to a cruel and ignominious death—yet through all and to the last, obedient and submissive to Him that sent him.

In this view, what follows is symmetrical and harmonious. "Wherefore" — because of this humility and obedience—"God also hath highly exalted him, and given him a name which is above every name." Mark you: Jesus hath not that name of himself, but it is the gift of God; how then can he be that God? "That at the name of Jesus every knee should bow, of things in heaven, and things in earth, and things under the earth; and that every tongue should confess that Jesus Christ is Lord, to the glory of God the Father." Had the Apostle intended to guard us against this very error, of supposing that he meant, when he said that Jesus was as our version reads. "in the form of God," that he was verily God — or that when he said he had received "a name which is above every name," he was verily the Supreme—how could he have done it better? He declares that his very "exaltation" is a reward; that his "name above every name" is a gift; that the homage he is to receive from all ranks of created beings, and the confession which is to be on their lips, are to be rendered and made to him as *Lord* and not as *God*, and expressly to or for "the glory of GOD the FATHER."

The highest Trinitarian authorities sustain our interpretation of this often quoted passage in all particulars. For example, as to the phrase, rendered in our English version, "in the form of God," Dr. Robinson in his Lexicon says of it, "i. e. as God, like God." As to the phrase "thought it not robbery to be equal with God," Dr. Whitby says, "did not covet to appear a God"; Bishop Sherlock—"was not fond, or tenacious of appearing as God"; Prof. Stuart—"He regarded not the being equal with God as a thing to be eagerly coveted." The last named critic says: "Our common version . . . . . seems to render nugatory, or at least irrelevant, a part of the Apostle's reasoning in the passage. He is enforcing the principle of Christian humility upon the Philippians . . . . But how was it any proof or example of humility, that *he did not think it robbery to be equal with God*"?*

Once more, we are referred to our Lord's own words to Philip: "He that hath seen me, hath seen the Father; and how sayest thou, Show us the Father?"†

* Answ. to Channing, p. 84. † John 14 : 9, 10.

Here, surely, is the highest possible and express testimony that Christ is God. To this I reply first, by a flat denial. Our Lord had no reference to the Divine Essence, but only to Divine excellences manifested in himself; to "works" which he had done, and which no man could do "except God were with him." Next, that he explains his language to Philip, in perfect consistency with language which he afterwards addressed to the "Father" as "the only True God."* He proceeded to say to Philip: "Believest thou not that I am in the Father and the Father in me? The words that I speak unto you, I speak not of myself; but the Father, that dwelleth in me, He doeth the works." So afterwards, addressing the Father, he says: "As thou, Father, art in me, and I in thee."† It was his consciousness of the *indwelling* God, speaking in his words, acting and operating in his miraculous and merciful works, that warranted him in saying: "He that hath seen me, hath seen the Father!" In a similar sense he had previously said: "He that seeth me, seeth Him that sent me!"‡ Only in that sense could Jesus have so uttered himself; for the same Apostle who in his Gospel records these declarations, says both in his Gospel and in his first Epistle: "No man hath seen God at any time."§ Besides all this, let any one read this entire fourteenth chapter of St. John's Gospel, nay, with it the two which follow; let him note how pointed is the distinction which Jesus makes between the Father as the source both of his wisdom and power, and himself;‖ let him note how careful he

* John 17 : 3. † John 17 : 21. ‡ John 12 : 45.
§ John 1 : 18; 1 Eph. 4 : 12. ‖ Vv. 10, 24, 28.

is to forbid his disciples praying to himself, but directs them to pray to the Father in his name;* let him, then, in immediate connection, read the seventeenth chapter, containing our Lord's remarkable prayer before his betrayal and arrest—yes, prayer—the very act and office expressive of inferiority and dependence; and unless his mind be wholly preöccupied by the influences of Trinitarian training, it would seem scarcely possible but that he should conclude, that whatever Jesus meant when he said, "He that hath seen me hath seen the Father," he assuredly did not mean that he was "the Invisible" God, "the blessed and only Potentate—the King of kings, and Lord of Lords—who only hath immortality; dwelling in the light which no man can approach unto; whom no man hath seen nor can see." Something else, something different from that, he must have meant; and that was, that in his life and character, his words and works, they beheld God most conspicuously and gloriously manifested.

I come now to a passage which is perhaps the one most readily cited against the Unitarian view of Christ, and which demands the fuller notice. I refer to the Proem or Introduction to St. John's Gospel.† That there is in it a degree of obscurity arising from our want of familiarity with the prevalent opinions of the time, may at once be admitted. To rectify and guard against the influence of these opinions, was in part the Apostle's object. On the one hand was the Jewish or later Platonism, the leader of which was the celebrated Philo Judæus, of Alexandria, and a cotemporary of our

* 16: 23, 26.

† John 1: 1–5.

Lord. On the other was Gnosticism, a heresy whose headquarters were at Ephesus; where, by the concurrent testimony of antiquity, the Apostle lived and wrote his Gospel. With the Gnostic opinions which prevailed throughout the regions of Greece and Asia Minor, where the new religion was spreading, the Apostle must, therefore, have been familiar; and Irenæus — a pupil of Polycarp, who was a personal friend and disciple of St. John, and who flourished early in the second century—declares that the Evangelist wrote expressly to confute them. Between the Neo-Platonic and Gnostic systems there were some coincidences. While the former made the Logos—the Divine Reason or Intellect, in the passage before us translated *Word*—to be the great instrument in Creation, and gradually extended its significance to comprehend all Divine attributes employed or manifested in the Creation and Government of the world, the latter made it the Chief of the Œons, supposed immortal spirits holding and exercising different functions or offices, themselves created, but still independent of the Supreme God. To correct these false notions was the purpose of the Apostle; by directing men's minds to GOD Himself, as the Great and Original Source of all things, the Creator of all beings, Himself independent, they all dependent on Him. In this sense the Logos—"the Word" (the Wisdom, Power, Reason of God—Divine attributes employed in the Creation and Government of the world) "was *with* God"; inherent, that is, in Him, of course;—"was God," because belonging to His essential nature. The syntax of the Greek language obliged him to seem at least to personify the

"Logos" or Word; to speak of it figuratively as a person; because the Greek noun is in the masculine gender, and therefore requires the personal pronouns in apposition with it to be in the same gender; whereas our English noun "word," by which it is translated, is in the neuter gender, and requires the neuter pronouns. Hence in the third verse of the passage under consideration it would be more agreeable to the English idiom to read "All things were made by *it*," etc. In another work by this same Apostle, that which he has here called simply *the Word*, he there, in the opinion of many commentators, calls *the Word of Life*, and *the Life*.* But while in the Greek *the Word* is masculine, *the Life* is feminine; consequently by neither expression could he have intended to designate a proper person, but used simply a figure of speech, a personification.

In all languages, ancient and modern, the Prosopopœia or Personification is a figure in frequent use. In the Book of Proverbs† there is a remarkable personification of *wisdom;* the corresponding word to which in the Greek translation or Septuagint, is that in St. John's Proem, Λόγος, *Logos*. A striking example occurs in the Apocryphal Book of the *Wisdom of Solomon*‡: "Thine Almighty *Word* leaped down from heaven from his royal throne, a fierce warrior, into the midst of a land of destruction." The author of this book lived at or a little before the time of Christ, and wrote in Greek; and was doubtless acquainted with the Neo-Platonism of the period. In the passage referred to

* 1st Ep. of John 1: 1, 2. † Ch. 8. ‡ 18: 15.

and in others,* the noun translated in our version *Word* is in the original, *Logos*. The same remark holds of a passage in another Apocryphal Book, "*Ecclesiasticus*";† where again we have a personification of *Wisdom* or *the Logos*, as in the passage cited above from "Proverbs." In all these cases the Greek term *Logos* has been by our translators rendered *Wisdom* or *Word* interchangeably, as though these terms were synonymous or equally significant.

But look further on. In the fourteenth verse the Apostle says: "The Word was made flesh and dwelt among us, full of grace and truth;" "dwelt" he means of course in Christ; in whom the Power and Wisdom of God were the credentials of his divine mission, and who was filled with God's own mercy and truth for the salvation of men. In a parenthesis he adds—"and we beheld his glory"—*underived* glory? No: "the glory as of *the only begotten* of the Father." Still more, with all that he has previously said, he proceeds in the eighteenth verse distinctly to affirm, that "no man hath seen God at any time; the only-begotten Son, who is in the bosom of the Father, he hath declared (revealed, made more clearly known, manifested,) Him."‡ Multitudes had seen Christ; and in Christ, His brightest manifestation, His chosen and anointed messenger and representative, they had seen in a high sense, in the only sense possible, the God who sent him.

* 9:1; 16:12, 13, 16. † 24:1, et seq.

‡ This 18th v. illustrates two passages before commented on, viz. John 14:9, 10 and 1 Tim. 3:16; supra pp. 98 and 109.

Yet once more. If St. John intended to teach that his Master was God, the Absolute, the Supreme God, would he not have said so plainly? Why use a circumlocution? Why all this ado about the Logos? Why not have continued to call him God throughout his Gospel, throughout his Epistles and Apocalypse, which he has never done? Why, on the contrary, write of him always as "the Son"—"the Son of God"—"the Son of Man"—"the Christ"? Nay, reverting again to the close of his Gospel, why did he not there, when summing up his labors, declare explicitly—"These are written that ye might *believe* that *Jesus is God*"—instead of, as he does—"These are written, that ye might believe that Jesus is the CHRIST, the SON of GOD; and that, believing," (believing that, believing so,) "ye might have life through his name"?*

"In the beginning" of all things—we may, then, understand the Evangelist to say—this vast creating Power and Wisdom was put forth. It "was with God"; inherently subsisting in and nothing separate from Him, the Great First Cause. "It was God"; no agent existing or acting apart from God; but essentially Himself; God exerting His active energy by and through His own Wisdom and Power, which "in the beginning" was inherent in Him, essential to His Godhead. By it were all things without exception created. It was the source or spring of all Life, the natural Light of all men. But this Light, before the Gospel was revealed, shone on a darkened world "which comprehended it not."—Thus interpreted, St. John

* John 20: 31.

obviously and most distinctly maintains the strict, simple, undivided Unity and Supremacy of God.*

Taking, then, these five verses of the first chapter of St. John's Gospel by themselves, it seems plain that he makes no personal reference, direct or indirect, to his Master. He aims, rather, to correct those false philosophic notions of his day, which either clashed with the great fundamental doctrine of all true religion, the doctrine of the Unity and Sovereignty of God; or which were but a veiled Atheism. When, however, we come to the fourteenth verse, we there find him asserting that the same Wisdom and Power by which God made the universe, "dwelt" in Jesus; so that he was lifted thereby out of the sphere of ordinary humanity; became a Divine Teacher; wielded superhuman Power; and by direct commission and authority from God, introduced and established in the world that holy religion of which John was his Apostle, and which is God's great and surpassing gift to the race.

I hold, then, that the doctrine of Christ's Supreme and proper Deity, is directly opposed by his own express words, and by those of his Apostles.—By his own: "And behold, one came and said unto him, Good Master, what shall I do to inherit eternal life? And Jesus said unto him, Why callest thou me good?

* "It is contended, indeed," says Prof. Norton, "that his words admit of a different meaning; that the Logos (Word) is here spoken of as a proper person; but that this person is, at the same time, declared to be, literally, God. But if we so understand St. John, his words will express a contradiction in terms. 'The Logos,' he says, 'was WITH God,' which, if the Logos be a person, necessarily implies that he is a different person from God. Whoever is WITH any being, must be diverse from that being with whom he is."—*Reasons*, etc. pp. 317, 318.

There is none good but One, that is GOD."* "Verily, verily, I say unto you, the Son can do nothing of himself. . . . I can of mine own self do nothing."† "My Father is greater than all."‡ "My Father is greater than I."§ It is pertinent to ask here, how do these, especially the two last, citations, correspond or harmonize with the alleged coëquality of the Three Persons of the Trinity?—By the words of his Apostles: "There is . . . one Lord, one Faith, one Baptism; One GOD and FATHER of all, who is above all, and through all, and in you all."‖ "There is *none other* God but One. For though there be that are called gods, whether in heaven or in earth, (as there be gods *many* and lords *many*,) but to us there is but ONE GOD, the FATHER, of whom are all things, and we in him; (or, "for him, i. e. to him our service and worship are due," as Mr. Locke interprets; or, "to whom we, as dependent creatures, belong," as Bp. Pearce.) "And One LORD, Jesus Christ, by whom all things" ("belonging to the new spiritual *creation* or dispensation—through whom the blessings and discoveries of the Gospel have been given,"¶) "and we by him," ("and by whom we have access unto the Father."**) "Then cometh the end, when he shall have delivered up the Kingdom to GOD, even the FATHER; when he shall have put down all rule and all authority and power. For he must reign till he hath put all things under his feet. The last enemy that shall be destroyed, is Death. For 'He hath put all things under his feet.'††

* Matt. 19 : 16, 17.
† John 5 : 19–30.
‡ Id. 10 : 29.
§ Id. 14 : 28.
‖ Ephes. 4 : 5, 6,
¶ Grotius.
** 1 Cor. 8 : 4–6.
†† Vid. Psalm 110 : 1.

But when he saith,* All things are put under him, it is manifest that he is excepted, which did put all things under him. And when all things shall be subdued unto him, then shall the Son also himself be subject unto Him who did put all things under him, that GOD may be all in all."†

Such language, surely, needs no explanation. It is clear, explicit, intelligible to the humblest reader. It is but a specimen of what we constantly meet in the New Testament. To hold to Christ's proper and Supreme Deity in the face of such direct testimony, nay, in the face of the whole tenor and drift of Holy Scripture, is, to say the least, amazing. It becomes nothing else, nothing more than a mere inference from some few and confessedly difficult texts. The Roman Catholic church has always insisted, bear in mind—and if this dogma is to be held at all, she is right—that so few and difficult are the passages of Scripture from which it is attempted to infer it, that the *traditions* of the Church are essential to prove it a part of Christian belief, and that it cannot be proved from Scripture without them. Nay, some of her most famous doctors have distinctly denied that it can even be inferred from Scripture, and rest it entirely on Tradition.‡

Who, then, is Christ? I will not dogmatize. This is not a question on which that would become me or any man. God has been pleased to keep some mystery

* "When it is said." Abp. Newcome.

† 1 Cor. 15 : 24–28.

‡ E. g. Masenius, Melchin Canus, Witsius; cited by Wilson, *Concessions*, etc., p. 51. Vid. also, H'y Taylor's "*Ben Mordecai's Apology,*" p. 46, et seq.

around it. If it be not so, what can we make of our Lord's positive declaration recorded in Luke and Matthew, "No man" (or, more conformably with our English idiom, *no one*) "knoweth *who* the Son *is*, but the Father"?* Surely there is that belonging to Christ, if words have any meaning, which no one but the Father knows.

Admit, then, that there is a degree of mystery surrounding this question, making it, perhaps, one of the things which, like "the times and the seasons" of which after his Resurrection our Lord spoke, "the Father hath put in His own power," and therefore "not for us to know" till He shall give us more light; what then? Other points, points of the highest practical moment and profoundest interest, are made perfectly plain, and stand out on the sacred page beyond all doubt or dispute by any who rest on the authority of Holy Writ. On that authority I profess to stand. On that authority I plant myself in this entire argument. I make no pretensions to being wise above what is there written. And, therefore, according to that Book which is to Protestants the common standard of revealed truth, I am ready and glad of the opportunity to make full and distinct confession of what I understand and preach as the Unitarian Faith.

I Believe, then, that Jesus is THE CHRIST. This I would emphasize. This of itself and alone is a great point. How remarkable that passage in the Gospels of Matthew, Mark, and Luke! "Jesus asked his disciples, saying, 'Whom do men say that I, the Son of

* Matt. 11 : 27; Luke 10 : 22.

man, am?' And they said, 'Some say that thou art John the Baptist; some, Elias; and others Jeremias, or one of the prophets.' He saith unto them, 'But whom say ye that I am?' And Simon Peter answered and said, 'Thou art THE CHRIST, the Son of the living GOD.' And Jesus answered and said unto him, 'Blessed art thou, Simon Barjona, (son of Jonah); for flesh and blood have not revealed it unto thee, but my Father who is in heaven.'" Our Lord is not content with simply approving Peter's declaration as true; he pronounces him specially blest in being able to make it, because resting on no mere human speculation, but on revelation from the Father. I call this a great truth; assuredly it is. If any single truth be fundamental in our religion, this is. It involves the veracity of our Lord himself. Deny it, and you deny him. It is the point on which he always insisted; and which, after his Ascension, was the turning point in the preaching of his Apostles. It is the connecting link between the Old and the New Dispensation. It is the result to which the long and golden thread of ancient Prophecy leads, and in which it ends. I am speaking, of course, of matters of strictly Christian faith or belief; and in such a connection recognize no hair-splitting between a *technical* and a *spiritual* Christianity. I well remember that the English Deists of the seventeenth and eighteenth centuries, like Lord Herbert of Cherbury, and others, at times spoke quite as respectfully of our Lord and of his religion as many of the modern rationalistic school in our own day. In the early part of the last century, Tindal entitled his Deistical attack upon Christianity, "Christianity as old as the Creation"; because, forsooth, as he argued, all truth being eternal, if Christianity contain truth, it can be no revelation or discovery. On the other hand, to deny Jesus to be the CHRIST, on the ground that that is *a mere Jewish idea never to be realized*, as has been recently done in our own vicinity, is only to evade the point at issue. No matter that the gross ideas which possessed the Jewish mind in our Lord's time were disappointed. He was all the more needed to correct those ideas, and lift the people from their grossness. The question is not whether he met the worldly and coarse expectations of the masses of his day, but whether he was the Predicted, the Promised Messiah, "the very CHRIST";* the specially Anointed Messenger and Representative of God; which last all Christendom always has affirmed and affirms still. "That we might believe that JESUS IS THE CHRIST, the SON of God,"† was the great purpose for which, as we have seen, St. John declares he had written his Gospel.

I believe that Jesus is the SON of God; not merely *a* son of God, as we all may be through that "glorious freedom" which is secured to us through the Gospel; not *a* son of God, as all intelligent beings are, according to our Lord's great revelation of the Fatherhood

* John 7: 26. The Greek adverb here rendered "very," in our Common Version, occurs previously in the same verse, and is there rendered "indeed"; and again in v. 40 of the same chapter, and is there rendered "of a truth." A good rendering would be by our English adverbs, *truly*, *really*. Griesbach, and after him Alford, rejects the adverb where it occurs the second time in v. 26. Then the passage would read, "Do the rulers *really* know that this is the Christ"?

† John 20: 31.

of the Supreme; but *the* Son of God in a high, special, peculiar, unrivalled sense; a title by which he is designated as holding a singular and most intimate relationship to the Father. This is elsewhere expressed by the phrases, "the only-begotten Son who is in the bosom of the Father"; "my beloved Son"; "the Son of God with power"; "him whom the Father hath sanctified and sent into the world."*

I believe him the one MEDIATOR; according to the words of St. Paul, who declares that "there is One God," also "One Mediator between God and man, the man Christ Jesus."† I thank God that there is. I bless God that He has provided for me—frail, weak, imperfect, tempted, erring, sinner as I am—this gracious channel of communication between Him and my soul. I confess, humbly yet joyfully confess the need. I know myself too well to decline or deny it.

I believe him to be our SAVIOUR—our compassionate, self-sacrificing, loving, all-sufficient Saviour. My soul gladly responds to that declaration of the same Apostle, "This is a faithful saying, and worthy of all acceptation, that Christ Jesus came into the world to save sinners":‡ and to that of the Apostle Peter: "Neither is there salvation in any other; for there is none other name under heaven given among men whereby we must be saved."§ "Him," whom "God hath thus exalted to be a Prince and a Saviour, to give repentance and forgiveness of sins,"‖ I confess and rejoice in, as "His unspeakable Gift."¶

* John 1: 18; Matt. 3 : 17; Rom. 1 : 4; John 10 : 36.
† 1 Tim. 2 : 5. ‡ 1 Tim. 1 : 15. § Acts 4 : 12.
‖ Id. 5 : 31. ¶ 2 Cor. 9 : 15.

Finally, I believe in Jesus as the INCARNATE WORD —"the Word made flesh."* In Jesus was the Divine Word or *Logos*;† which qualified him for his great mission; which constituted him the most illustrious Representative and Manifestation of God—in the glowing language of the Epistle to the Hebrews, "the brightness of God's glory, the express image of His person";‡ which made his words the words of God, his works the works of God; which inspired him with superhuman wisdom, clothed him with superhuman powers, took him utterly out of the category of ordinary humanity, placed him far above all previous Prophets and Messengers from God, and gave him rank second only to the Supreme in His moral universe. I gratefully acknowledge and bow to his Authority. In my profoundest religious consciousness, I regard his words as of the same binding force as though they were uttered evidently and audibly to me from the opened heavens by the Almighty Himself.

But in saying all this, remember, I "confess him" only "Lord, to the glory of God the Father."§ I dare not say less; for there is his own emphatic declaration: "Whosoever shall confess me before men, him will I confess before my Father who is in heaven. But whosoever shall deny me before men, him will I also deny before my Father who is in heaven."‖ How confess him, if not in the very offices he claimed?—I dare not say more; assuredly, I dare not say aught which shall seem as far as words can to dethrone God, aught which

* John 1: 14. † Vid. supra, pp. 103–104, etc. ‡ Heb. 1: 3.
§ Philipp. 2: 11. ‖ Matt. 10: 32, 33.

shall seem to derogate from the essential, underived, unrivalled Supremacy of the Father. I know that I am required to "honor the Son, even as I honor the Father";* but in this connection I also know that I can honor the Father rightly and justly, only by receiving and honoring the Son as His Minister and Representative, in precisely those Offices and Relations in which it has pleased God to place and reveal him. I should dishonor God, nay, I should dishonor the Son, by attempting any thing more.

Herein may be seen, that Divinity of Christ which the Unitarian Church affirms; not his Deity, for that is another matter, and that it denies. Christ *is* Divine, but He *is not* GOD. His Divineness or Divinity, is because of his intimate, peculiar, in some degree even, mysterious, union with the Father; because of his Offices, Powers, Gifts; because that "in him dwelt all the fulness of the Godhead bodily";† and because he is thus "Head over all to the Church."‡

Such in this respect, I understand to be Unitarian *Christianity*, or, *Christian* Unitarianism. It is the faith which, with unshaken, unwavering, increasing confidence that it is the truth of God, I for more than thirty years have preached; the faith in which I rejoice to live, and hope to die. Any thing less in regard to our Lord Jesus Christ, I do not acknowledge to be Christian Unitarianism; or, indeed, any thing less to be Christianity. I accept, I hold as dearer than life, Christianity as a Revealed Religion, a direct and express Revelation "from the Father of lights." In the

* John 5 : 23. † Col. 2 : 9. ‡ Eph. 1 : 22.

limited sense of Monotheism, there are various forms of Unitarianism. It may be Deism, Rationalism, Naturalism; all virtually the same thing; and all alike rejecting the idea of Revealed Religion, and whatever puts forth the claim. It may be Judaism, resting on the Divine Legation of Moses. It may be Mohammedanism falsely alleging Mohammed to be *the* Prophet of God, It may be Hindooism, which, according to Ram Mohun Roy's translation of the Veds, the Hindoo Scriptures, teaches the doctrine of One God. All these, being as I have said, Monotheism, are so far Unitarianism. But I am speaking of and for CHRISTIAN Unitarianism: which not only recognizes and adores One GOD, the FATHER, but one LORD, JESUS the CHRIST;* bearing on its forefront the plain and explicit words of that Lord himself, addressed in solemn prayer to that Father; "This is Life Eternal, to know THEE, the Only True GOD, and JESUS the CHRIST whom Thou hast sent."†

1 Cor. 8 : 6. † John 17 : 3.

LECTURE VI.

DOUBLE NATURE OF CHRIST—PERSONALITY AND DEITY OF THE HOLY GHOST.

I FIND myself unexpectedly, and before entering on the main theme of my present Lecture, obliged* to turn aside for a moment, and consider another. It is one on which I had deemed it scarcely necessary to spend breath, namely, the Doctrine, as it is theologically called, of the Double Nature of Christ, or the Hypostatic Union. The argument from Scripture is very limited. Besides two passages already fully commented on,† namely, the Proem of St. John's Gospel, and a passage in the Epistle to the Philippians, there are but two others on which it has even the shadow of a foundation. Both occur in the Epistle to the Romans. In the first chapter‡ St. Paul has these words: "His Son Jesus Christ, our Lord, which was made of the seed of David, according to the flesh; and declared to be the Son of God, with power, according to the spirit of holiness, by the resurrection from the dead." In the ninth chapter:§ "I could wish myself accursed from

* By a respectful letter of inquiry received after delivery of the last Lecture.

† John 1 : 1–18, supra, p. 111. Phil. 2 : 6, supra, p. 107.

‡ vv. 3, 4. § vv. 3, 5.

Christ for my brethren, my kinsmen according to the flesh. . . . Whose are the fathers, and of whom as concerning the flesh, Christ came, who is over all, God blessed forever." The closing part of this second passage, I have already commented upon in another connection.* Now remember, that the allegation of our Trinitarian brethren is, that Christ had two distinct and complete natures, Divine and Human; in the one he was God, in the other, Man. The question before us now, therefore, is, whether these passages sustain the allegation? It is made a question, bear in mind, as to *nature;* and because St. Paul, in the first, uses both the expressions, "according to the flesh," and "according to the spirit of holiness," with reference to our Lord—the one as being "of the seed of David," the other as being "the Son of God with power"—here is proof, it is said, of his possessing two natures. But turn to the second passage. There you find the Apostle using the same phrase, "according to the flesh," in regard to himself, in its obvious sense, without the least reference to any peculiarity of *nature*, which, of course, in his case, will not be pretended; but simply to the matter of descent from the common stock of all Israelites, by virtue of which he shared with them "the promises." Why not, then, to Jesus, who, by universal consent, was "of the seed of David," and therefore of "the fathers," the patriarchs and founders of the nation; "of whom, *as concerning*" (the phrase in the Greek is the same, *according to*) "the flesh," i. e. by natural descent, he "came," and in correspondence with prophecy, must have come?

* Vid. supra, p. 95.

There is no reasonable pretence for understanding the phrase rendered "according to the flesh," and which is of frequent and invariable use elsewhere by St. Paul in his Epistles,* with reference to natural descent, in any other sense in either passage. It cannot be interpreted with reference to his human, in contradistinction from his divine nature, except to make out a case, to support this mere hypothesis. Paul declares, that he "had been called to his Apostleship, to preach the Gospel of God, concerning his Son Jesus Christ, our Lord, (how carefully he distinguishes them!) who, he says, by natural or lineal descent, was of the house of David; but by the Holy Spirit was demonstrated to be the Son of God, with power, by his Resurrection from the dead."† Thus I paraphrase the first passage, to show its true meaning.

The other argument is drawn from the alleged necessity of the case. Christ is sometimes called God, and sometimes Man. This must be explained. Here is a mystery, and it must be solved. From this supposed necessity springs the hypothesis of the Double Nature in Christ. "This," says Wardlaw,‡ "is the key which fits all the wards of this intricate lock, turning among them with hardly a touch of interruption, catching its bolts, and laying open to us, in the easiest and

* E. g. 1 Cor. 10 : 18.

† With St. Paul, the RESURRECTION of Christ was the final, crowning proof of his Sonship and Messiahship. Acts 13 : 30–37 ; 17 : 31 ; Rom. 6 : 4 ; 10 : 9 ; 1 Cor. 15 : 15, etc. Paul is always careful to attribute it to the "power" of God, to the act of God himself, and not to any independent power in our Lord.

‡ Discourses on the Socinian Controversy, p. 44, Amer. ed.

completest manner the treasures of Divine Truth." To this I simply answer, that we do not find the lock, and therefore we do not want the key; or the mystery, and therefore we do not want the solution. To us no such necessity, as is alleged, exists. The hypothesis is entirely uncalled for. Nothing is plainer than that there is not the remotest hint of any such thing as a twofold nature in Christ, in all his recorded words, or in the writings of his Apostles; though it is hardly possible that they should have been silent on so grave a point, had there been in it any reality. Regarding it then as the merest hypothesis, for that is all it is, we object, aside of its superfluity, that its admission makes difficulty where there is none; renders vague or obscure the plainest and most explicit language of Scripture. It demands on its face the surrender of reason, and involves positive absurdity. Divine and human qualities, as the essence of being, cannot co-exist in the same person. God is infinite, man is finite; and no being can be at once and essentially finite and infinite.* It estops inquiry by its plea of mystery; and drives us, would we believe it, to the old position of Tertullian: *Credo quia impossibile est*, (I believe because it is impossible.) It destroys Christ's unity, and makes

* "As before, of the doctrine of the Trinity, so now of the doctrine of the Hypostatic Union, as it is called, I ask for a single hint throughout the New Testament of the inconceivable fact that, in the body of Jesus, resided the mind of God and the mind of man—two natures, the one finite, the other infinite, yet making but one person—a difficulty you will perceive the very opposite of that of the Trinity; for whereas that teaches three persons in one nature, this teaches two natures in one person."—Rev. J. H. Thom, Liv. Lect. 7th Unitarian Lec. p. 72.

him two distinct and opposite beings. That Christ is both God and man, is a proposition plain enough in its statement; but the two predicates are incompatible. But a graver objection is, that in effect it charges our Lord with duplicity. When he declared on one occasion: "Of that day and hour knoweth no man; no, not the angels which are in heaven, neither the Son, but the Father"*—what more precise and significant words could he have used, to show that he laid no claim to Omniscience, that attribute essential to Deity, without which no being could be God? If there was any one thing of which our Lord was ignorant, he could not be God. And how should we have understood him, had we been present—how did the Apostles, how did the multitude who were present, understand him at the time? They must have understood him as we do, to have made a positive, express declaration, that "of that day and hour" he had no knowledge;† and therefore to suppose that he made a mental reservation, as to his divine knowledge, while he declared only his human want of it, is to charge him with duplicity, with double-dealing, with deceit.

Hence we object, again, that it lessens the force of his example. Surely the least imputation to Christ, if there be reason for it, of any such quality as deceit,

* Matt. 13: 32.

† The force of our position cannot however be evaded in this case by the hypothesis in question; for our Lord's words are too comprehensive. "No man," as I have already elsewhere observed, excludes his own "human nature"; "neither the Son," his divine nature: for "the Son" is alleged to denote *God the Son*, or specifically the divine nature of Christ, in virtue of which he is God.

must have that effect. But on this hypothesis, what mean all his declarations of dependence on God? "Of mine own self I can do nothing; as I hear, I judge; and my judgment is just, *because* I seek not mine own will, but the will of the Father which hath sent me"; just as he had before said: "The Son can do nothing of himself, but what he seeth the Father do."*—What mean his expressions of trust in God? To Pilate's haughty menace he replied, "Thou couldest have no power at all against me, except it were given thee from above"; and in that most solemn hour when he was drawing his last breath upon the cross, he said: "Father, into thy hands I commend my spirit!"† To whom were these words addressed? To whom was he accustomed to pray? To one part of his nature—to himself—to a part of himself? What mockery all this seems! Finally, this hypothesis conflicts with all just principles of interpretation. "It is reasonable to expect, that those doctrines which form the leading articles of any system," says Dr. Wardlaw,‡ "should be plainly stated in the book which professes to make that system known." Apply this test to the doctrine—for sheer hypothesis as it is, it is alleged to be not only one but a "leading article" of Christianity—to the doctrine, then, of the two natures in Christ; and who will pretend that it is "plainly stated" in Scripture? But, for the obvious principle that Scripture is to be interpreted like any other book, we have the high orthodox authority of Prof. Stuart, and of other orthodox

* John 5: 19, 30. † John 19: 11; Luke 23: 46.
‡ Disc. on Soc. p. 223.

critics of equal eminence with him. "If there be," he says, "any book on earth that is addressed to the reason and common sense of mankind, the Bible is preëminently that book. . . . . If the Bible is not a Book which is intelligible in the same way as other books are, then it is difficult to see how it is a *revelation* . . . . . the Bible is addressed to our reason and understanding and moral feelings; and consequently we are to interpret it in such a way as we do any other book that is addressed to these same faculties."* These principles and the rule they involve, are inevitably violated by this hypothesis. By its admission, the Bible cannot be interpreted like other books. Plain language in other books is taken in its plain significance; but here the plainest becomes a riddle. When our Lord says, "My Father is greater than I," he meant only that his divine nature was greater than his human nature! But who can prove that he so meant? Neither he nor his disciples, give the slightest reason to suppose that he or they meant any thing but what their words obviously mean. Besides, we cannot tell when to apply the hypothesis. We are all in the dark; and the Scripture may be made to mean by it the most contradictory things. Whatever Christ said or did may thus be done away, and the entire New Testament become a mass of enigma.

I come now to the main theme of the present Lecture, viz: The Personality and Deity of the Holy Ghost. And, to begin, what is precisely this doctrine of

* Biblical Repos. vol. ii. pp. 129, 130.

the Holy Ghost or Holy Spirit, which Unitarians reject? In the 5th of the thirty-nine "Articles of Religion" of the Protestant Episcopal Church, we read, that, "The Holy Ghost, proceeding from the Father and the Son, is of one substance, majesty, and glory with the Father and the Son, very and eternal God;" conformably with the 1st Article: "In unity of the Godhead, there be three persons, of one substance, power, and eternity; the Father, the Son, and the Holy Ghost."

In the 3d sect. of the 2d chap. of the Presbyterian Confession of Faith, we have really the same statement, closing with—"the Holy Ghost eternally proceeding from the Father and the Son." In the Athanasian Creed, it is said: "There is one person of the Father, another of the Son, and another of the Holy Ghost. But the Godhead of the Father, of the Son, and of the Holy Ghost, is all one; the glory equal, the majesty co-eternal . . . . In this Trinity none is afore or after other, none is greater or less than another. But the whole three Persons are co-eternal together and co-equal." In the Nicene-Constantinopolitan Creed: "I believe in the Holy Ghost, the Lord and Giver of Life, who proceedeth from the Father and the Son; who with the Father and the Son together is worshipped and glorified, who spake by the prophets."

It will be seen at once that there are two branches of the doctrine as thus stated; the first, Personality, making the Holy Ghost a Person; the second, Deity, making it God. To sustain the popular or orthodox belief, it must be proved, then, that the Holy Ghost is a Person. But, not to quibble about the impropriety and unnaturalness of attributing without proof personality to that, which both in Greek and English is named by nouns in the neuter gender,* how is its personality supposed to be proved?

The first passage to which I refer, as offered for this purpose, is in the first Epistle to the Corinthians: "The Spirit searcheth all things, yea, the deep things of God."† To "search," is an attribute of a Person, or a personal attribute; therefore, the Spirit is a Person. But this reasoning proves too much; for in the next verse the Apostle thus proceeds: "For what man knoweth the things of a man, save the spirit of man which is in him? Even so, the things of God knoweth no man, but the Spirit of God."‡ To "know" is a personal attribute; therefore the "spirit of man" is a Person.—Is it? Assuredly the language of Paul proves it to be, quite as conclusively as the "Spirit of God."

Again: "Wherefore, as the Holy Ghost *saith*, 'To-day, if ye will hear,'" etc.§—The writer to the Hebrews quotes from the ninety-fifth Psalm; and the words quoted are the words of the *Psalmist.* Turn to the second epistle of Peter,‖ and the matter is all explained: "For the prophecy came not in old time by the will of *man*, but *holy men of God* SPAKE as they were moved by the Holy Ghost." The Psalmist was one of these "holy men of God," and "spake" as he was "moved by the" Spirit of God.

Again: "Why hath Satan filled thy heart to lie to

* Gr. Πνεῦμα, *Pneuma*—Eng. *Ghost* or *Spirit.* † 2 : 10.
‡ 1 Cor. 2 : 11. § Heb. 3 : 7. ‖ 1 : 21.

the Holy Ghost? Thou hast not lied unto man, but unto God!"* What proof is there here of *distinct* personality? This passage is one, in which the terms *Holy Ghost* and *God* are, as occasionally elsewhere, used synonymously; in other words, the phrase Holy Ghost is here and elsewhere used to signify God Himself; precisely as we speak of a man's spirit as the man himself, without the remotest hint or idea of more than one person.

In John's Gospel the question is supposed by Trinitarians to be put entirely at rest. "I will pray the Father, and He shall give you another Comforter, that he may abide with you forever, even the Spirit of truth; whom the world cannot receive because it seeth him not, neither knoweth him; but ye know him, for he dwelleth with you, and shall be in you . . . . . But the Comforter, which is the Holy Ghost, which the Father will send in my name, he shall teach you all things . . . . . When the Comforter is come, whom I will send unto you from the Father, even the Spirit of truth, which proceedeth from the Father, he shall testify of me . . . . If I go not away, the Comforter will not come unto you; but if I depart, I will send him unto you, and when he is come he will reprove, etc. . . . . . When he, the Spirit of truth is come, he will guide you into all truth; for he shall not speak of himself," (i. e. of course, not of his own suggestion), "but, whatsoever he shall hear," (i. e. whatsoever shall be communicated to him), "that shall he speak," etc.†

Now in the first place, what marvellous language

* Acts 5 : 3, 4. † John 14 : 16, 17, 26; 15 : 26; 16 : 7, 8, 13

this, for one co-equal God to use of another co-equal God! The whole is incompatible with co-equality. But, on the Trinitarian hypothesis there are *three* co-equal Gods; and yet the second promises to pray to the first, and then he will give the third. In one place it seems that the first will send the third in the name of the second; and then, that the second will send him from the first. And then, again, the third will not come while the second is here, and not till he sends him after his own departure. Moreover, when the third comes, to be a guide into all truth, his ability is not inherent, not underived, but dependent on the communications he may receive.

Again, it is to be remarked, that throughout, "the Holy Ghost"—"the Comforter"—"the Spirit of Truth," are all synonymous phrases, or titles, interchangeably used of the same subject.

Next, that in each case where either is used, there is a plain distinction from GOD—from *the Father*, who *is* God.

And, finally, this being so, that which is thus distinguished from God, cannot be God; and since God is necessarily alone Supreme, it must be subordinate to and dependent on Him. Accordingly, it is said to be *sent from the Father*, to *proceed from* the Father, to be sent at the instance of *Christ praying to* the Father.

The truth is, that, at the most, there runs through these entire extracts from our Lord's farewell discourse, a rhetorical *prosopopœia* or *personification* of the Holy Spirit. And yet, perhaps, hardly so much as that, when we consider the structure of the Greek language and the necessities of its syntax. To explain: the

Greek pronouns, relative and personal, have distinct genders, and terminations marking these genders; and in use take of course the gender of the nouns to which they are applied. "The Comforter" is in Greek a masculine noun, and should have masculine pronouns. But "the Comforter" is "the Holy Spirit;" and "Spirit" is a neuter noun, and should have neuter pronouns. This rule is strictly adhered to in the original; but not in our version, where in one of these extracts the neuter noun "Spirit," is followed by the personal instead of neuter pronouns.* In the Rev. L. A. Sawyer's new Translation—heralded by so many orthodox trumpets—this error is corrected; and there the passage thus reads as it ought—"the Spirit of truth, which the world cannot receive, because it beholds *it* not, nor knows *it;* but you know *it*, because *it* continues with you and shall be in you." It is plain, then, that the use of the personal pronouns does not here prove personality in the subject to which they are applied; for the synonym here used for "*the Comforter*," which, being masculine, has the masculine pronouns, is "the Holy Spirit;" which, though neuter, has in our version the masculine pronouns.

Still more; if the use of pronouns is to determine this question, then the Greek original viewed as a whole, conclusively decides against the alleged personality of the Holy Spirit. The words Holy Ghost, Holy Spirit, (both, in Greek, the same phrases,) the Spirit, the Spirit of truth, occur more than a hundred times in Scripture; always in the neuter gender, of

* John 16 : 14

course; always, of course, with corresponding neuter articles, adjectives, participles, pronouns; not once, therefore, is the Holy Ghost spoken of in all these times as a *person* but a *thing*. In this discourse of our Lord occurs the only exception; and this, where he gives the Holy Spirit the new title of "the Comforter," using a Greek noun of the masculine gender, and so of necessity or design, or both, so far personifying it. Yes, this is a solitary exception; it stands alone; and may have been, as already said, a mere matter of necessity by reason of the Greek syntax. Taking it, however, in its strongest aspect, as a designed personification, it is only of figurative significance and certainly proves no personality. The single exception cannot destroy, but rather, proves the rule. The single passage, or class of passages, where the figurative expression was used on a single occasion, cannot control the more than a hundred literal and plain ones.

Besides, "the promise" of "the Comforter" was renewed *after* the Resurrection of the Lord, but the personification was dropped. "Behold," he said, "I send the promise of my Father upon you; but tarry ye in the city of Jerusalem, until ye be endued with power from on high."* Luke, who records this in his Gospel, in the opening of the Acts † alludes to it, and makes our Lord say—"Ye shall be baptized with the Holy Ghost . . . . ye shall receive power, after that the Holy Ghost is come upon you." "The promise" is sufficiently explained then, by the phrases "endued with power from on high"—"baptized with the Holy

* Luke 24 : 49. † 1 : 4, 5, 8.

Ghost"—"receive power." It was fulfilled at Pentecost, when we read that "they were all *filled with* the Holy Ghost, and began to speak with other tongues as the Spirit gave them utterance"; and more distinctly and in direct reference to this, Peter said on that occasion—"Jesus . . . . being by the right hand of God exalted, and having received of the Father *the promise* of the Holy Ghost, hath shed forth *this*, which ye now see and hear."* But *how* was "the promise" fulfilled? Were the assembly "filled" by a "Person"; or, by a mighty influence and inspiration? By the coming of a "Person"; or, by wondrous symbols and gifts?

These texts exhaust the Scriptural argument. The Holy Ghost or Spirit, is not a Person; is not God, except as the phrase is sometimes used to denote Him, the Supreme. That the terms Holy Ghost, Holy Spirit, Spirit of God, Spirit, are thus used, both in the Old and New Testaments, no one denies.† Taken, however, as the names of a third person of the Trinity, he cannot be, even according to the Creeds as we have already seen, self-existent, underived, unoriginated, of independent being, which God must be; for they, so far following Scripture, declare that he *proceeds from* the Father, who confessedly *is* God; and, therefore, he is subordinate to Him, the Supreme. But they have not even the least color of being names of a "Third person" or of any person, with the single exception above stated. Most commonly and significantly, they

* Acts 2 : 4, 33.

† Job 33 : 4; Ps. 139 : 7; Acts 5 : 3, 4, 9; 15 : 28.

are used to denote certain powers, gifts, influences, aids, supernaturally imparted by the Deity to the Prophets,* to Christ,† to the Apostles, and the converts to the early Church, whether Jews or Gentiles.‡ The "devout" Watts, whose hymns, written during his Trinitarian days, are the staple of most English and American "collections," says in his "Faithful Inquiry," "the Holy Spirit in the New Testament, when it speaks of things after the ascension of Christ, very generally, or for the most part means, that *power or influence* of the eternal Spirit of God, which *proceedeth from the Father.*"§

That this view is the true one, and comprehends the full Scriptural idea, follows from the common expressions of Scripture in this connection. The Holy Spirit is said to be "shed upon" men‖—to be "poured out" upon them¶—to be "given" by God**—to be received as a gift.†† Men are said to be "filled with," "full of," the Holy Ghost.‡‡ "If," says Dr. Watts, "the Holy Spirit were really a true and proper person, it would be difficult to account for all these, and as many more expressions of Scripture, which cannot possibly be ascribed to a proper person; and if in some places these impersonal expressions, or in other places the personal expressions, must be figurative, why may not

* Old Testament everywhere. † Matt. 12 : 28; Luke 1 : 15.

‡ Acts 2; id. 11 : 15, etc.

§ Faithful Inquiry after the ancient and original Doctrine of the Trinity, p. 30.

‖ Tit. 3 : 6. ¶ Acts 10 : 45. ** John 3 : 34; 1 John 4 : 13.

†† Acts 2 : 38; 8 : 17. ‡‡ Acts 2 : 4; 11 : 24; 13 : 52. See Isa. 11 : 2.

my explication of them do as well as the contrary? And thus the Spirit of God need *not anywhere* be construed *into a real, proper, distinct person*."*

The Holy Ghost is personified—what then? Personification is a figure of speech; and by it any thing may be made to appear, so far as language is concerned, a person. We constantly use it, in familiar, as well as in solemn discourse. The Holy Ghost *is* personified, and that is all; being only personified, it is not a Person, any more than is "the Law"† which is said to be *speaking;* or "the Scripture" (the Old Testament)‡ which is represented as *foreseeing* and *preaching;* or Sin,§ which is described as *deceiving* and *slaying;* or Charity,‖ because so beautifully personified by St. Paul. Remarkable instances of the personification of Wisdom were cited in the last Lecture, from the Proverbs and the Apocryphal Books of the Old Testament. Is Wisdom, therefore, or the Law, or Scripture, or Sin, or Charity, each a Person? And if the Holy Spirit be personified as the Comforter, as teaching, speaking, testifying, reproving, why any more should it be regarded as a distinct Divine Person—or still more, as God from all eternity?

Ram Mohun Roy, having shown the strange and repulsive results which must follow in the interpretation of Scripture from the principle of making the Holy Ghost "a third distinct person of the Godhead, equal in power and glory with the Father of all," closes with this striking remark: "Still more dangerous to true

* Faithful Inquiry, p. 30. † Rom. 3 : 19. ‡ Gal. 3 : 8.
§ Rom. 7 : 11. ‖ 1 Cor. 13.

religion would it be to interpret, according to the Trinitarian mode, the passages which describe the descent of the Holy Ghost upon Jesus on the occasion of his baptism. Luke, ch. 3 ver. 22 : 'And the Holy Ghost descended in a bodily shape like a dove upon him.'— For if we believe that Spirit, in the form of a dove, or in any other *bodily shape*, was really the third person of the Godhead, how can we justly charge with absurdity the Hindoo legends of the Divinity having the form of a fish or of any other animal ?"*

We demand to know what good reason can be assigned for the remarkable silence of our Lord and his Aportles upon this point, if indeed it be true, or a required part of our Christian faith ? Assuredly, they never say that the Holy Spirit is a *person* distinct from God, or a third person of the Godhead. If it be a distinct Divine Person, to be separately worshipped as verily God, why have they not so told and so directed us ? Never, not in a single instance, are we taught by them to worship the Spirit. On the contrary, Jesus directs us to worship the Father,† and his own example is uniformly consistent with that direction.‡ He in-

* 2d *Appeal*, p. 234. As a specimen of Ram Mohun Roy's reasoning alluded to above, he says: "If the term 'Holy Ghost' be synonymous with the third person of the Godhead, and 'Christ' with the second person, these passages may be read as follows: 'He, the second person, shall baptize you with the third person of the Godhead, and with fire.' [Luke 3 : 16.] 'God anointed Jesus of Nazareth (the second person of the Godhead) with the third person of the Godhead, and with power,'" etc. etc. See 2d *Appeal*, pp. 232–234; indeed, the whole of chap. 6.

† E. g. John 4 : 23, 24 ; Matt. 6 : 9.

‡ E. g. Matt. 11 : 25 ; John 17.

structs us to ask the Father for the GIFT of the Spirit.* How carefully do he and his Apostles distinguish the Spirit as "the Spirit of GOD"!† "The Spirit" is never joined with "the Father" and "Son" in the very places where it were most natural to expect it would be, if it were intended we should understand or interpret it according to the Trinitarian theology. For example, our Lord, in solemn prayer to the Father, says: "This is Life Eternal, to know Thee, the only true God, and Jesus Christ whom Thou hast sent."‡ I lay stress on these words. Can it be supposed that he did not know whom he thus addressed? Not a word is said of, no allusion is made to, the Spirit. Throughout the prayer, full and prolonged as it is, this holds true. Remark, then, that he, the SON, that same Jesus of whom he himself speaks as—not God—not "God the Son"—but the CHRIST, "sent" of the Father, addresses that FATHER as the ONLY TRUE GOD. I feel that I might well content myself with this, so emphatic, so explicit is the language; so memorable the occasion when it was used, when, if ever, he would speak as the case demanded; when he would declare who was the ONLY TRUE GOD; and as is the fact did declare that THE FATHER was HE.

Take other examples from the introductory salutations of St. Paul's Epistles. To the Romans: "Grace to you, and peace, from God our Father, and the Lord Jesus Christ." To the (2d Ep.) Corinthians: "Grace be to you, and peace, from God our Father, and from the Lord Jesus Christ. Blessed be God, even the Fa-

* Luke 11: 11. † Matt. 12: 28; Rom. 8: 9, 14; 1 Cor. 2: 11.
‡ John 17: 3.

ther of our Lord Jesus Christ"—mark this language—"the Father of mercies, and the God of all comfort." To Titus: "Grace, mercy, and peace, from God the Father, and the Lord Jesus Christ our Saviour." See how distinctly the Father alone is recognized as God; and how in each case no mention is made of, no reference is had to, the Spirit. Without a single exception, this is true of all these introductory salutations in the Pauline, while there is nothing but what is in entire harmony with them in the other Apostolic Epistles: as for example, in the second of St. John, we read: "Grace be with you, mercy, and peace, from God the Father, and from the Lord Jesus Christ, the Son of the Father."* Nay, in his first Epistle John says: "Truly our fellowship is with the Father, and with His Son Jesus Christ."† Is it to be believed that these inspired Apostles, knowing that there was a Trinity of Persons in the Godhead—"God the Father, God the Son, and God the Holy Ghost"—should, nevertheless, in every case, not only thus carefully distinguish between the Father and the Son; but in every case, style the Father alone GOD; so emphatically make the Son, *His* Son; and all the while utterly ignore the Holy Ghost?

Look, moreover, at those solemn charges which St. Paul gave to Timothy his "own son in the faith." "I charge thee before God, and the Lord Jesus Christ, and"—(the Holy Ghost? No. But)—"the elect angels."‡ "I give thee charge in the sight of God, who quickeneth all things; and before Christ Jesus, who before Pontius Pilate witnessed a good confession · that

* See, also, 1 Pet. 1: 2, 3.

† 1 John 1: 3.

‡ 1 Tim. 5: 21.

thou keep this commandment without spot, unrebukable, until the appearing of our Lord Jesus Christ; which in His times HE shall show who is the Blessed and Only Potentate, the King of Kings, and Lord of Lords; who only hath immortality, dwelling in the light which no man can approach unto; whom no man hath seen nor can see: to whom be honor and power everlasting. Amen."* Not only is the same distinction preserved in both passages, on which I have remarked before, between the Father as GOD, and Christ as LORD; but in the last, the Apostle, as if for the very purpose of keeping before the mind of Timothy the unchallenged and absolute Supremacy of the One God the Father, breaks forth into a glowing and sublime description of Him, and yet makes no reference to or mention of the Holy Spirit. Why did he not, in those introductory salutations above recited, in these charges thus solemnly given, speak of Christ as "God the Son," instead of Lord, if such he knew or believed him to be? Why did he not charge Timothy *before* "*God the Holy Ghost*," as well as before the other august names there named, if such he knew or believed the Holy Ghost to be? There can be but one answer. He neither knew nor believed the one or the other.

Finally, the history of this doctrine of the Personality and Deity of the Holy Spirit condemns it. For nearly four centuries it was scarcely dreamed of; it had no place, certainly, in the "Christian consciousness" of the mass of believers. It was a thing of time, and of degrees, because the doctrine of the Trinity of which it is a part, was such. "The desire of

* 1 Tim. 6: 13–16; vide also, 2 Tim. 4: 1.

bringing the doctrine of the Trinity *to a conclusion*, led *gradually* to more definite views on the personality of the Holy Ghost." So says Hagenbach, writing of what was accomplished during what he styles "The First Period" of the history of the church or from A.D. 80 to A.D. 254.* Could any language better illustrate the fact, that not upon clear Scripture testimony, but upon the arguments of polemics, and the decrees of councils, this doctrine was built? "The subject of the personality and divinity of the Holy Spirit," says Prof. Norton—and his testimony, after his profound study of the subject is not lightly to be set aside—"was in a very unsettled state before the Council of Constantinople (A.D. 381.)"† "A hundred and fifty bishops," says Mosheim, "who were present at the Council, gave the finishing touch to what the Council of Nice (A.D. 324) had left imperfect; and fixed, in a full and determinate manner, the doctrine of *three* Persons *in one* God."‡ He had previously said:§ "The subject of this fatal controversy, which kindled such deplorable divisions throughout the Christian world, was the doctrine of *three persons* in the Godhead; a doctrine which in three preceding centuries"—he is writing of the *fourth* century—"had happily escaped the vain curiosity of human researches, and been left undefined and undetermined by any particular set of ideas."

Here we may leave the subject. The History of

* Hist. of Doctrine, vol. i. p. 125. † Statement, etc. p. 43.

‡ Mosheim's Eccl. Hist. vol. i. p. 326.

§ Id. p. 314. See also, Muenscher's Dogmat. Hist. (Murdoch's Transl.) p. 60. Sparks' Letters to Wyatt, p. 181.

the Church on its dogmatic side, shows the origin of this doctrine to have been any thing but Scriptural. The New Testament, in Mr. Wardlaw's words, "the book which professes to make the Christian system known," is on this subject silent; is, by the showing even of orthodox critics of the highest repute, at least very reserved upon it. Our Lord, in what may be reverently called his *definition* of that, which, as knowledge, at least, really secured "Eternal Life," entirely omitted it. And, although there can be no Trinity in the modern orthodox sense without it, what an ominous silence to a very great degree is there in Trinitarian pulpits and works respecting it! How little is heard, how little in our day is written, about it! Does not a strong presumption against it hence arise?

The discussion of the Trinity closes with this Lecture. As Unitarians we reject the dogma of a Tri-Personal God, as a monstrous fiction. We believe, as firmly and gratefully as any of our Christian brethren of any branch of the Universal Church, in the Father, in the Son, and in the Holy Ghost—the simple and only Trinity of the Apostolic age and the First ages of the Church. It is not the province of any who may differ from us to deny that we do, merely because of that difference. "To his own Master, each standeth or falleth."—The Holy Ghost, what is it but the Spirit of God? And as we say that the spirit of a man is the man himself, so we may say that the Spirit of God is God Himself. But more commonly it is to be regarded as that holy influence by which God, our heavenly Father, moves upon, renews, and sanctifies the hearts of His children; aids them in difficulty, strengthens them in temptation, prompts them to repentance, comforts them in sorrow, inspires in them noble resolve, nerves them for high moral action, and quickens them in duty. "In the name of the Father, of the Son, and of the Holy Ghost," we baptize the adult believer, and the infant of the believer, as commanded by our Lord; nor can we ask or pronounce any higher blessing for ourselves or for others, than what is expressed in the significant words of the Apostolic benediction: "The Grace of our Lord Jesus Christ, the Love of God, and the Communion of the Holy Ghost, be with you all!"

LECTURE VII.

HUMAN NATURE.

WHAT is the doctrine which I am to oppose in this Lecture? The 9th Article of Religion of the Episcopal Church declares, that "Original sin standeth not in the following of Adam, but it is the fault and corruption of the Nature of every man, that naturally is engendered of the offspring of Adam, whereby man is very far gone from original righteousness, and is of his own nature inclined to evil, so that the flesh lusteth always against the Spirit; and therefore in every person born into this world, it deserveth God's wrath and damnation."

In the sixth chapter of the Presbyterian Confession we read that "By this sin ('of our first parents') they fell from their original righteousness and communion with God, and so became dead in sin, and wholly defiled in all the faculties and parts of soul and body. They being the root of all mankind, the guilt of this sin was imputed, and the same death in sin and corrupted nature conveyed to all their posterity, descending from them by ordinary generation. From this original corruption, whereby we are utterly indisposed, disabled, and made opposite to all good, and wholly inclined to all evil, do proceed all actual transgressions."

Accordingly we find an English Episcopal Divine saying: "Yes, man is a ruined creature, under the practical dominion of his carnal affections and appetites . . . . . . In the day that Adam sinned, you and I sinned, and our children sinned, and their children who are yet unborn sinned; for all men sinned while as yet there was only one man. Adam stood as the head of the whole human race: while he was holy, all were holy in him; while he was innocent, all were innocent in him; when he fell, all fell in him; when death passed on him, death passed on all; when he became alienated from the love of God, so as to hide himself in terror, we all became alienated; when he deserved hell, so did we all."*

So an eminent Presbyterian clergyman of the neighboring metropolis says: "By the doctrine of the imputation of Adam's sin, many of the Reformers meant that innate moral depravity of heart, and consequent condemnation, which came upon all his posterity by his first offence. This appears to me to be the doctrine of Native Depravity. . . . . By the wise appointment of God, this primitive sin constituted all his posterity sinners. When he fell, prospectively considered, they fell; and from the moment of his apostacy, the entire race, of every age and every condition, down to the last infant that should be born on the earth, rose up to the view of the divine mind, as lost and ruined by their iniquity. Such is the condition to which the first apostacy introduced the race. . . . . It is not

* Rev. H. McNeile, M.A., of Liverpool, Eng., 7th Lect. on the "Unitarian Controversy," pp. 297, 303.

necessary for us to do any thing to ruin our children; they are ruined already . . . We consecrate our children to God (in baptism), not because they are incapable of moral action—not because they are innocent—but because they are *sinners* . . . . . Nor is my native depravity my misfortune merely, but my fault. Sure I am that I stand condemned at the bar of conscience and at the bar of God, for my native depravity."*

That these statements are not universally accepted by orthodox theologians, I gladly admit; and hail the fact among the symptoms, already too many to be ignored, of a great advance in the orthodox body towards more just and liberal views. The late Professors Stuart of Andover, and Taylor of New-Haven, really came to the decision that infants are incapable of sinning. Nay, "the New-Haven Divinity," as it was commonly and often by its orthodox opponents contemptuously called, and of which the "Christian Spectator" was the expounder, taught views on a part of this subject thirty years ago, largely approaching in some of its statements those of Unitarians; and they were met by the writer in the Dissertation from which I last quoted, and by others, with unsparing condemnation. He there characterized those views as "both false and dangerous," and "the spirit with which they were disseminated" as "a bold and vaunting spirit." They are now widely received and constantly preached by many prominent men in various orthodox denominations. The Old and New Schools of the

* Rev. Gardiner Spring, D.D., Dissertation on Native Depravity, pp. 19, 20, 90, 92.

orthodox Congregational and Presbyterian Churches, and the Low Church and High Church in the Episcopal body, are respectively wide apart in their teaching on this subject. With the more liberal, rational, and Scriptural views in some respects held by the latter upon it, we have little controversy; while we deem those of the former so false, irrational, and unscriptural, that we shall do battle with them to the last. Still they who in those churches hold the truer views, so long as they accept and defend the dogmatic statements of their Articles, Confessions and Creeds, notwithstanding all their explanations or criticisms, must be held responsible for the errors which those Articles, Confessions and Creeds perpetuate. They should not be allowed to think they can shelter themselves under those explanations and criticisms. By the Articles, Confessions, and Creeds, to which they subscribe, or belief in which they profess, and which are published to the world, as the dogmatic basis on which their Churches rest, must the faith of those Churches be tried.* Now on no point of Christian doctrine, is it of more practical importance that right views should prevail, than on this before us. The old Calvinistic doctrine of Native Depravity, Original Sin, is traceable to Augustine, early in the fifth century of the Christian era. No single mind has exerted a more decisive influence on the theology of Christendom as to this

* Consult Barnes' Introd. Essay to Butler's Analogy, pp. xxxv., xxxviii., xxxix; Prof. Stuart on the Romans, particularly Exc. 5; Chr. Spectator for June, 1829, p. 348, et al.; Chr. Examiner, vol. ix. pp. 220–227; Spring on Native Depravity, passim.

point, in connection with the whole popular theory of redemption by Christ. And no single corruption of the pure doctrine of the Gospel, has kept a more tenacious hold on the Church, or been of more baleful effect, than this of which he is the author.

There are obviously two branches to the orthodox doctrine of Human Nature: — 1. the imputation of Adam's sin; 2. the total corruption of Human Nature, as the consequence of Adam's fall. The first, is virtually yielded by the New School Calvinists as they have been called; but the second seems, at least in words, clung to still. "The *imputation of Adam's sin to his posterity*," said Dr. Woods, "in any sense which those words naturally and properly convey, is a doctrine which we do not believe"; and again: "Every attempt, which has been made, to prove that God ever imputes to man any sinful disposition or act, which is not strictly *his own*, has, in my judgment, failed of success."* The only wonder is, that the "attempt" should ever have been made. Yet before this, he had stated "the doctrine which the Orthodox in New-England hold" on the second branch of the subject to be—"*that men are by nature destitute of holiness;* or that they are subjects of an *innate moral depravity;* or, in other words, that they are from the first inclined to evil, and that, while unrenewed, their moral affections and actions are wholly wrong."† The Italics in these extracts are in the original; I certainly have no disposition to contradict the position in the last extract, "that men *are* by nature destitute of holiness." It is, so far as it

* Letters to Unitarians, pp. 44, 45. † Id. p. 31.

goes, strictly Unitarian, and no Unitarian will deny it. But, in the same breath to say, "that they are *subjects of an innate moral depravity*"; or, much more, by the phrase "in other words," to try to make it appear to be synonymous with saying, "that they are *from the first* inclined to evil"; nay, "that *while unrenewed*, their *moral affections and actions* are *wholly wrong*"; is not only an entirely different matter, but simply monstrous. What is it, in reality, but a re-assertion of the Old Calvinism; or, if not, and meant as a substitute for it, where is the gain?—So the late Dr. Taylor of New-Haven said: "A ground of certainty exists in the mind of each individual of our race, that the *first* and *all subsequent acts* of moral agency, will *uniformly be sinful, previous to regeneration*." And Prof. Stuart said: "I admit that all are born in such a state, that it is now certain they will be sinners as soon as they are moral agents . . . . . they are in such circumstances that *they will all sin as soon as they are capable of sinning*, and never do any thing holy until they are regenerated. . . . All came into the world in such a state, as makes it *certain* that their *appetites, which lead to sin, will prevail;* and they never will have any holiness, until they are born again."* These distinguished men opposed as firmly as Dr. Woods, the doctrine of "the imputation of Adam's sin to his posterity"; and then, offered this "modern substitute for a Sinful Nature," as it was styled in an admirable paper by the late Dr. Noah Worcester.† To such statements, Dr. Ware of Cam-

* Stuart's Comm. on Rom. pp. 240, 242, 526.

† Chr. Examiner, vol. ix. N. S. p. 219.

bridge, in reply, well stated the Unitarian position thus: "Man is by nature—by which is to be understood, as he is born into the world, as he comes from the hands of his Creator—innocent and pure; free from all moral corruption, *as well as* destitute of all positive holiness."*

Taking, therefore, the Orthodox view in its least objectionable statement, as a whole, it seems presumptively, irreconcileable with the character of God as a Father, as that is declared and illustrated in the Gospel. No good parent, least of all the impartial and All-perfect Father, whom Christ has brought near to our religious faith and love, could thus regard his children. In the case of God however, he is not only their Father, but their Creator; and in both relations His character must be harmonious. To have created, nay, to continue to create, for centuries past and for unknown centuries to come, a race of beings, who "will be sinners as soon as they are born"—of whom it is "certain that their 'first' act of moral agency, 'previous to regeneration,' will be sinful, and that their appetites which lead to sin, will prevail"—making them thus "liable to all punishments in this world and that which is to come"†—is, I repeat, utterly inconsistent with the Parental Character of the Almighty, as portrayed by the Saviour; nay, with all our natural conceptions of a Just and Righteous God. If this argument be not conclusive against that view, it assuredly is enough to re-

* Ware's Letters to Trinitarians, p. 20.

† "Larger Catechism," Ans. to Quest. 27.

strain us from accepting it, except upon unquestionable Scriptural authority.

So, again, the doctrine is in itself repulsive. The human mind instinctively revolts at it. And this being so, the very fact suggests, that with a mind so sensitive, the moral nature of man cannot be so corrupt. If God our Creator has implanted within us a natural sense of right and wrong, that sense arraigns His character and conduct in creating us thus corrupt.

All observation and experience contradict the view under consideration. Dr. Spring, who holds, indeed, the extreme doctrine of his Church on this subject, only follows out, after all, to their legitimate result, the principles of orthodoxy, when he says: "What reason have we for *solicitude on account of our children!* They are *born in sin.* They partake of the same sinning, corrupt nature with their parents. From the crown of their heads to the soles of their feet, they are *full of wounds, and bruises, and putrifying sores, that have not been bound up, nor mollified with ointment.* Their *hearts are full of evil,* and in them *there dwelleth no good thing. They are estranged from the womb; they go astray as soon as they are born, speaking lies. Their poison is like the poison of a serpent.* It is as natural for them to sin, as it is for the sting of a serpent to be poisonous. They are under the wrath and curse of God, and there is no redemption for them but through the propitiation of his only Son. What spectacle is more affecting than an immortal being entering upon its only probation, with such a character! Every time you look upon a little child, or a sleeping infant, you see — what? An apostate sinner—man fallen — human nature in ruins! When you clasp your fond babe to your bosom, well may solicitude and compassion find a dwelling within your heart. With all those lineaments of intelligence, and of beauty and amiableness, they are *dead in sin.* That warm heart that trembles and beats at your side, 'beats iniquity and death.' Ah! how often have the interest and pride of many a gratified parent been turned to tenderness and tears, as she bore her endeared offspring in her arms, and recollected that it is the *child of wrath, even as others.*"* Mothers! this is addressed to you. Whose of your hearts responds to such an appeal as true? Did I not know that the now venerable author was a sincere, devout, and exemplary Christian minister, I should suppose this mere poetry; albeit belonging rather to the Satanic school than to that founded on the Gospel. As it is, it furnishes but another striking and grateful illustration of how much better a man may be than his creed.

After all, the great point at issue is, not whether there is such a thing as human depravity, a great deal of it, for no one denies that: but, whence came it? Not, whether men be depraved, for they *are* greatly; but how do they become so? The question really is, being corrupt, being depraved, are they born corrupt, does God bring them into the world depraved? Admit that men are in the highest conceivable or possible degree depraved, it would by no means follow, that there was any original, inherent moral taint. Violent passion, brutal excess of appetite, foul intemperance,

* Dr. Spring on Nat. Depravity, pp. 87, 88

self-indulgence, selfishness, violated rights, injustice, fraud, pride, oppression, slavery, war, and a thousand other bad things or bad traits there may be, and yet no original taint or incapacity. But I deny that in the main, mankind are as bad as represented. There is current and gross exaggeration on that point. On the contrary, there is more virtue than vice; more goodness than wickedness. The one is retired, noiseless, modest; the other, bold, noisy, rude. Nothing is easier, than by partial or exclusive coloring, to make the picture bright or dark. You may bring into a single view all conceivable vice, all conceivable virtue. Test the popular doctrine by Infancy. If there be any marked characteristics of infancy, they are simplicity, artlessness, freedom from everything deserving suspicion, veracity, innocence, purity. Marks enough there are of helplessness, weakness, dependence, but none of duplicity or malignity. With scarcely an exception, infancy is interesting. What a wondrous concession is that of Prof. Stuart, that "all men pronounce infants to be innocent, until theory bids them contradict this."* But surely, were Calvinism true, this could not be.

Holy Scripture warrants no such theory, no such belief, as the popular theory, the orthodox belief. The general drift of the sacred volume is the other way. Its commands, its warnings, its threatenings, its precepts, its exhortations, its promises, are all by necessary implication opposed to it. They cease to have force, they fail of meaning or justness, upon such a basis. Why command, why warn, why threaten, why

* As quoted by Dr. G. Spring, in "Native Depravity," p. 71.

direct, why exhort, why promise, an already wholly corrupt, depraved, disabled being?

But how, specially, did our Lord treat and regard human nature? When his disciples rebuked parents for presuming to bring "little children" to him for his blessing, what did he say? "Suffer little children, and forbid them not to come unto me, FOR *of such is the kingdom of heaven*."* Nay, before that, how emphatic had been his words! The disciples asked: "Who is the greatest in the kingdom of heaven? And Jesus called a little child unto him, and set him in the midst of them, and said—'Verily I say unto you, except *ye* be converted, and become as little children, ye shall not enter into the kingdom of heaven! Whosoever therefore shall humble himself as this little child, the same is greatest in the kingdom of heaven.'"† I rather think our blessed Lord knew of what he thus affirmed; and with what glorious force of meaning it would ring on the ears of his hearers, and reach the unsophisticated heart of humanity through all time. St. Paul, too, the very Apostle who is charged with portraying human nature in the blackest possible colors, when he is only describing the shocking degeneracy prevalent in portions of the heathen world,‡ thus exhorts his Corinthian converts, living in the midst of one of the most corrupt communities of ancient Greece—"in malice be ye *children*," as though that were the last thing to be found in *them*.§ The ignorance of children he recognizes — "be not

* Matt. 19 : 4; Mark 10 : 14; Luke 18 : 16. † Matt. 18 : 1–4.
‡ Rom. 1. § 1 Cor. 14 : 20.

children *in understanding;* howbeit *in malice* be ye children." The Apostle clearly thought a good deal better of children, than that they were totally depraved or born in sin.

It is not, indeed, so much as pretended that the doctrine of Human Nature against which we contend is expressly declared in Scripture, but rather that it is of necessity to be inferred from its frequent language. For example we are pointed to such texts as this: "And God saw that the *wickedness* of man was great on the earth, and that every imagination of the thoughts of his heart was only evil continually."* As though this were a description of Human Nature, instead of human character! Where is the first hint in it of a corrupt nature, of hereditary total guilt, of innate aversion to holiness as a thing born in man? "Wickedness" there was, and it was great; but the very word "wickedness" implies something very different from an inherent taint, or the outbreak of positive moral inability. So in the Psalms,† when David, brought by the faithful rebuke of God's prophet into the profoundest penitence for his outrageous crimes, gives vent to his penitential emotion in the poetry of passion, we are called upon to regard him at the very time as an inspired oracle of Divine truth deliberately giving a statement of it! And when Jeremiah, having expressed in the strongest terms the wretchedness of trusting in man, and the blessedness of trusting in God, sets forth the reason in this emphatic language‡— "The heart is deceitful above all things, and despe-

* Gen. 6 : 5. † Ps. 51 : 5. ‡ Jerem. 17 : 9

rately wicked"—we are bound to accept this as a literal description of man by nature! Now at the most, it describes a too common characteristic of men; but nothing is hinted as to its origin; nor does it follow that however common, it is positively universal. Nay, the contrary inevitably follows from the very next verse: "I the Lord search the heart—even to give *every* man according to *his* ways, and according to the fruit of *his* doings." That great Apostle, too, to whom I referred a moment ago, cannot be suffered to quote the poetic and hyperbolic language of the Old Testament, the literary as well as sacred treasure-house of his nation, and apply it for illustrating his position that the Jewish and Heathen or Gentile world were alike "under sin"—not under "*native depravity*" either partial or total, but under *sin*, which I take to be a personal and not an inherited or imputed matter—but lo, we must receive the language as a strict, literal, philosophical statement in regard to human *nature*, instead of a loose, popular, poetic picture of human *character*, and that of individuals or men of a particular era!* Refer to the Psalms from which the Apostle quotes, and you will see, that, notwithstanding the Psalmist represents God as finding "*none* that doeth good, no, *not one*," he still finds occasion to contrast "the *workers of* iniquity" with "my people," i. e. God's people; to speak of "the generation of the righteous"; of "the poor" whose "refuge is the Lord." Is it not plain, that he had no idea of being understood literally in his previous words? Just as Paul himself, when he

* Rom. 3 : 10–18; see also Ps. 14 and 53.

says in reference to the Gospel of Christ—"the grace of God that bringeth salvation hath appeared unto *all men*"—or when he spoke of it as "preached to *every creature*"—doubtless knew and felt that they to whom he wrote would appreciate the proper significance of his hyperbole; the most natural mode of expression on a momentous theme to the Oriental mind.

But this way of citation from Scripture, is sometimes even further strained to make out a case for our brethren on the opposite side of this subject. They insist that we must take the worst characters in Scripture history* as types of human nature, of man universally; characters like Pharaoh or Saul or Jeroboam or Judas as individuals; like Sodom or Canaan or Jerusalem in their worst days as communities. Instances and examples of marked and monstrous wickedness, by which to judge the nature which the entire race of man brings into the world! Could any thing be more absurd? Then we must pass by and ignore Moses, however pious, humane and meek, and think only of the cruel and obstinate monarch of Egypt; pass by and ignore the conscientious, public-spirited, unselfish, generous, devout Josiah, and think only of the ambitious, selfish, unprincipled Jeroboam; pass by and ignore every good and noble quality in David, and think only of his confessed and bitterly repented, however monstrous crimes; nay, pass by and ignore the gentle, true, and Christ-like John, and the other ten, who, however wavering at first, were to the last loyal, and think only of the wretched man who could

* Vid. Dr. Woods' Letters to Unitarians, pp. 38, 39.

for a paltry sum betray to his enemies and to a cruel death, the Innocent, nay, "the Holy One and the Just," his Master and best Friend! Against this mode of testing Human Nature, that nature which God has given us, I most earnestly protest. It is a libel on the Creator. As to its reasonableness, we might as reasonably test the health of a community by going to its Hospitals and Lazar-houses, and singling out cases of the worst possible types of disease.

Turning now to the New Testament, it is alleged that the doctrine under review, is of necessity implied by our Lord's words to Nicodemus: "Except a man be born again, he cannot see the kingdom of God."* Not so, for the universal need of Regeneration is entirely consistent with the primitive innocence of every man. The natural birth gives no moral character; that is to be formed; and when formed, is well called a new birth. The necessity of a new or spiritual birth is quite as conceivable on the supposition of native purity as of native sinfulness, of original innocence as original sin. The Saviour meant only but most distinctly to declare, that by natural birth we do not possess any positive moral character; that negatively we are by nature simply innocent, neither good nor bad; that the character essential to his disciple, to a true Christian, is a righteous and holy character which must be sought and achieved. So, too, when Paul says, "All have sinned,"† who doubts or denies that? All *have* sinned. It is a mere assertion of a fact; but without imputation or the remotest hint of hereditary

* John 3 : 3, 5.

† Rom. 5 : 12.

guilt or original sin. Again, he says to the Ephesians: "We...... were by nature children of wrath, even as others."* "By nature," or more according with our own idiom, "naturally," i. e. by the condition and circumstances into which by birth, whether as Jews or Gentiles, they were introduced. Very much as in another place Paul says—"We, who are Jews *by nature*," naturally or by natural birth, "and *not* sinners of the Gentiles."—"Children of wrath," then? These words are no proof of hereditary moral corruption, either total or partial. They have no reference to a natural but an acquired state; to no corruption of "nature," i.e. natural constitution, but of habits and conduct. Speaking of the state of all men, Jews and Gentiles, previously to their reception of Christianity, he says that in that condition, so corrupt were they, they were "children of," deserving of, "wrath." By impurity, licentiousness, sin, they had made themselves such. How can the opposite or orthodox view of the passage be reconciled with the passage in Romans, where the same Apostle argues, that "when the Gentiles, which have not the law, do *by nature* the things contained in the law, these, having not the law, are a law unto themselves; which show the work of the law written in their hearts"?† Could a nature totally corrupt prompt its possessor to "do the things of the law" or lawful things? Besides, in the passage specially under consideration,‡ the Apostle proceeds to compare the *natural* condition of the Ephesians, with that into which the Gospel had brought them. In that

* Chap. 2 : 3. † Rom. 2 : 14, 15. ‡ Ephes. 2 : 3, etc.

natural state they were "dead in sin—without Christ—aliens from the commonwealth of Israel—strangers from the covenants of promise—far off—having no hope—without God in the world—strangers and foreigners." This they were "by nature," or, in their natural *condition*. But "by grace," "the grace of God which bringeth salvation,"* they had been "made nigh by the blood of Christ—quickened together with Christ—raised up—made to sit together in heavenly places—fellow-citizens with the saints, and of the household of God." He says nothing of their corruption or depravity of nature or constitution; but seems to have thought no language too strong to express the inestimable advantages they now enjoyed, and the awful degradation from which they had been delivered.

I have now examined the chief Scriptural authorities, relied on for the support of those views on this subject, which we reject. Among them all there is not a word of our Lord himself except what he said to Nicodemus, which is cited therefor. So little of Scripture is there, on which with the least plausibility to found this startling doctrine of the "corruption of man's nature, whereby he is utterly indisposed, disabled, and made opposite unto all that is spiritually good, and wholly inclined to all evil, and that continually";† or, according to the Episcopal "Articles of Religion," which teach that "Original sin . . . is the fault and corruption of the nature of every man . . . whereby man is very far gone from original righteous-

* Titus 2 : 11.

† Assembly's Larger Catechism, Ans. to Quest. 25

ness, and is of his own nature inclined to evil, so that the flesh lusteth always contrary to the spirit; and therefore in every person born into this world, it deserveth God's wrath and damnation."*

But not only is it unscriptural, which with Unitarians is alone an all-sufficient objection to it; it is utterly inconsistent with the moral character of the Creator, as unfolded in Scripture—a perfectly just and holy and gracious Being. He gave us our nature, be it what it may. It is of no moment to say, that the depravity of our nature consists in its actual corruption, or only in inevitable tendencies to corruption; or to urge, that our disability is not the want of physical or natural ability, but the want of moral ability; not the want of power, but the want of will; a distinction attempted by the modern Calvinistic school. In either case the depravity, the corruption, is inevitable; and therefore neither censurable nor punishable by a just God. Guilt implies both will and power, both moral and natural ability. If the effectual influences of the Holy Spirit be needed, if without them there be no hope, and if in any case they be withheld, there is then no guilt on the part of man. If "some men are predestinated unto everlasting life, and others foreordained to everlasting death"; if the one, "being fallen in Adam" like all the rest, are nevertheless "effectually called unto faith in Christ, by His (God's) Spirit working in due season;" and "the rest of mankind, God is pleased . . . to pass by, and ordain to dishonor and wrath for their sin," it is worse than idle to talk of this being

* Art. ix.

"to the praise of His glorious justice"—it is mockery!*—God's "glorious justice," indeed! Who implanted in us the sentiment of justice but He? The most arbitrary government on earth would be execrated, should it thus act, thus treat its subjects, under the name or pretence of that sacred attribute. And yet men have been for ages, and still are too largely, expected to admire and extol in the Almighty, what they execrate and denounce in their own race!

The doctrine in question is inconsistent with all our natural, human, parental feelings. What parent who really believed it, could consistently look complacently even, not to say joyously and gratefully, on his child? How would he dread to think of himself as instrumental in giving that child being! Fortunately for the peace of parents, few really believe—they only imagine, possibly say—they believe it. It is the language of their Confession, or Catechism, or Creed, and they adopt it. The doctrine, moreover, clashes with all virtuous aspiration. It is soul-crushing, degrading, withering. Were all men in fact thus depraved, thus corrupt, either in the one sense or in the other above referred to, whence all the undeniable virtue, all the undeniable goodness in the world? If none but the regenerate can will or do a good deed, then surely all are already regenerate and sanctified; for who so bad, so depraved, as never to will or do a good deed? Such a monster in human shape does not exist.

To account for the origin of sin in man, there is no need of going beyond the obvious facts of his moral

* See Presbyterian Confession of Faith, chaps. iii. and x.

nature, and the present state of trial, probation, preparation, in which he is placed. A moral nature is a free nature; its possessor has freedom of choice and will and action; and trial or probation can alone put such a being or such a nature to the test. Accordingly we read in Scripture, that "God hath made men upright, but they have sought out many inventions."

As to the claim so often made for orthodox views of human nature, that they are essentially humbling views, and thus especially tend to foster that great Christian grace, Humility, while those which we hold tend to foster Pride, none could be more baseless. Which views are most likely, I ask, to make a man humble —those which teach him, that his sin is the inevitable, inherent growth of a nature from the start depraved; or those which teach him, that it is the result of a careless or wilful perversion or corruption of a nature given to us innocent and pure? The former, consistently held, must lessen the consciousness of personal guilt, or of the essential evil of sin; but the latter show that evil in its true light; make sin the moral abuse or neglect of great faculties, opportunities, and privileges, the deliberate, wilful breach of the commands of the best of beings, our God and Father; and thus stamp it beyond evasion or escape with an enormity, which must humble an awakened sinner to the dust.

Do you now ask, what, explicitly stated, is the Unitarian view of Human Nature—*our* nature—at birth and in infancy, I reply in our Lord's own words: "Of such (little children) is the kingdom of heaven." We believe—nay, we *know*, as certainly as we know any moral fact, and because we know that God is a perfectly just as well as gracious Being—that man by nature, man as born and brought into this world, is innocent, pure; guiltless because sinless; fitted for just that religion which Christ revealed to operate successfully and gloriously upon; not indeed holy, but capable of becoming so. When the period of moral responsibleness is reached and entered—a period which with exactness is known in any supposed case only to God—as we find none perfect, the character becomes a mixed one, in part good, in part bad, varying in countless varieties of shades and degrees. In every case, however, the wickedness, depravity, sin on the one hand, or the goodness, excellence, virtue, on the other, is one's own, of his own will, of his own purpose, of his own act. Personal guilt, personal desert, personal accountableness, that is, were else out of the question. Even *after* what is technically called "the Fall," it is written in Genesis,* that "in the image of God made He man;"—in the Psalms†: "Thou hast made him (man) a little lower than the angels, and crowned him with glory and honor:" and by Paul, that "a man . . . . is the image and glory of God."‡ Yes, Paul, the Apostle of the Gentiles; who is so often alleged to be the inspired teacher of this tremendous dogma of man's innate total depravity and original sin.

Man, then, in and by the nature which God has given him, is a being of glorious, God-like affections and faculties; and hence we speak, and most justly and by divine warrant as we confidently believe, of the glory, the grandeur, the dignity of that nature. None

* 9 : 6. † 8 : 5. ‡ 1 Cor. 11 : 7.

the less do we shut our eyes to the appalling fact of man's actual and great depravity and sin. Why, that very word *depravity*, on its face implies a corruption, a depravation of what was originally, as we received it at the hand of our Maker, pure; and such depravity, alas! we every where see. We profoundly feel that sin is no light thing, but in a high sense the greatest, most real and fearful evil of all. We acknowledge as gratefully, as devoutly as any, that to redeem us from sin, Christ "came forth from the Father and came into the world." We do not condemn men in the gross, nay, we do not condemn all notorious sinners, even, without mercy, for God does not. We have learned from the highest authority to "judge not"—at least not superficially or hastily. To the All-Seeing there may appear in every—the worst—case, circumstances of palliation, of extenuation, which we cannot see. The convicted pirate, the highway robber, the midnight murderer, the worst felon in your prisons—how happens it that you or I are not in his place? How many untoward circumstances and influences—misdirected or wretched education, early bad associates, a Godless home—circumstances and influences which you or I might have no more resisted than he, drove him there? What know we, as a thing of personal experience, of life in the purlieus of these great cities, with its homelessness, its squalid misery, its filth and noisomeness, its haggard and reckless vice, its mighty, ceaseless torrent of evil and malignant power? Yet even there, I doubt not, and therefore hesitate not to say, might be found some goodness; at least some germ, some material, that could be made to unfold and bear fruit—some spark, faint, and well-nigh dying, that could be kindled up—on which to work. The sainted Tuckerman, who inaugurated our blessed "Ministry-at-large" in Boston; the later years of whose life and labors were almost exclusively given to the poor, the outcast, the prisoner; when his hope had almost gone, as he reasoned and appealed and prayed in the cell and the ear of a hardened felon, found the ice melt and the iron soften, at the spell of that single word—"Mother"!

I conjure you, cherish ever a high rather than a low view of your nature. Sin is not the normal condition of the soul, but its saddest perversion and corruption. We were not made for that, but to be holy; faithful doers of the Divine will; co-workers with God and with His Christ. What significant attestation to the native innocence and native rectitude of our human nature did our Lord give, when he described so strikingly the prodigal in his repentance, as "coming to himself"!

LECTURE VIII.

THE ATONEMENT.

In the orthodox catalogue of Christian doctrines, that of the Atonement is probably regarded by most of those who accept it, as of paramount importance. I have found it not unfrequently the case, that where the hold on the Tri-personal Trinity has been abandoned, that on the Atonement remained almost as tenacious as ever, notwithstanding the logical cohesion of parts in the system was infallibly broken. I should be the last to deny, indeed, that the questions connected with the discussion of this doctrine, are among the gravest which can be started; or that it is at all strange, that minds trained under orthodox influences should so reluctantly reject it, or even admit doubts concerning it. The subject properly understood, comprehends, beyond question, the very essence and purpose of the Gospel. But, when it is claimed that the doctrine, in the precise form held by any of the orthodox, nay, by any church or body of churches in Christendom, is an essential doctrine; essential, that is, to a true faith in Christ, or to salvation, that we at once and explicitly deny. It is an arrogant and impertinent claim, be it put forth by whom it may. It is a violation of the Christian "law of liberty," the right of individual, private judgment, against which we shall always protest. Besides, were it in either sense essential, it should, nay, it would be one and uniform; there would be no difference of opinion about it, no liability to err in the way of understanding it; it would be capable of being so stated, that no mistake or misapprehension should be possible to any honest, inquiring mind.

But it is not so. On the contrary, no doctrine is more variously, in more multiform and opposite ways stated and expounded, by the creeds or the preachers or the writers that teach it. I must ask your patience while I give you some proofs of this position.

The thirty-first "Article" of the Episcopal Church declares that—"the offering of Christ once made, is that perfect redemption, propitiation, and satisfaction, for all the sins of the whole world, both original and actual; and there is none other satisfaction for sin, but that alone." It will be observed that neither here, nor throughout the "Book of Common Prayer," in any of its prescribed forms, does the word *Atonement* once occur; although so much is said and written of the doctrine usually called by that name, by the theologians and divines of that church.—The same remark is true of the Presbyterian Confession of Faith, which in the 4th sect. of chap. viii. says: "This office (of a mediator, etc.) the Lord Jesus did most willingly undertake; which, that he might discharge, he was made under the law, and did perfectly fulfil it; endured most grievous torments immediately in his soul; and most painful sufferings in his body; was crucified and died." And in the 3d sect. of chap. ix. says: "Christ, by his obedience and death, did fully discharge the debt of all those that are justified, and did make a proper, real, and full satisfaction to his Father's justice in their behalf."

Mr. Wardlaw says, that the leading object of Christ's mediation was, "to render the exercise of God's mercy, in bestowing free forgiveness, consistent, in the eyes of his intelligent creatures, with the claims of his dishonored authority, the demands of his justice, the glory of his holiness, the rectitude of his moral administration, and the general good of his Universe."*

Archbishop Magee says: "The sacrifice of Christ was never deemed by any who did not wish to calumniate the doctrine of Atonement, to have made God placable, but merely viewed as the means appointed by the Divine Wisdom, through which to bestow forgiveness." And a little further on he adds—"the notion of the efficiency of the sacrifice of Christ contained in the doctrine of Atonement, stands precisely on the same foundation, with that of pure intercession —merely as the *means*, whereby God has thought fit to grant his favor and gracious aid to repentant sinners, and fulfil that merciful intention, which he had at all times entertained towards his fallen creatures."† Again, he says‡ he uses "the expression, vicarious *import*, rather than *vicarious*, to avoid furnishing color to

* Disc. on Socinianism, p. 185.

† Magee on the Atonement, vol. i. pp. 18, 19.

‡ Ibid. p. 268. Illust. No. xxxviii.

the idle charge, made against the doctrine of Atonement, of supposing *a real substitution* in the room of the offender, *a literal translation* of his guilt and punishment to the immolated victim; a thing utterly incomprehensible, as neither *guilt* nor *punishment* can be conceived, but with reference to *consciousness*, which cannot be transferred." Perhaps no writer has been more lauded or quoted by the orthodox than this very one; none ever expressed himself more bitterly than he upon Unitarianism, and in this identical work; and all the while, he here sets forth his own views in a form, which he ought to have known had in the general statement always been held by a very large portion of those whom he condemned. Indeed Mr. Sparks declares, that "no language could better express the general faith of Unitarians."*

Bishop Butler says: "Christ offered himself a propitiatory sacrifice and made atonement for the sins of the world.—This sacrifice was in the highest degree, and with the most extensive influence, of efficacy in obtaining pardon of sin.†

Prof. Stuart maintains that Christ "suffered as our substitute; or, that his sufferings and death were an expiatory offering on account of which our sins are pardoned, and we are restored to the divine favor."‡ But Prof. Murdoch, in a totally different strain, says: "The Atonement was an *exhibition* or *display*. That is, it was a *symbolical transaction*. It was a transaction

* Sparks' Lett. to Miller, p. 210. † Anal. of Rel. p. 266.

‡ Discourses on the Atonement, as quoted in Unit. Miscellany, vol. vi. p. 310.

in which God and his Son were the actors; and they acted in perfect harmony, though performing different parts in the august drama. The Son in particular, passed voluntarily through various scenes of humiliation and sorrow and suffering; while the Father looked on with all that tenderness and deep concern, which he—and none but he—could feel. The object of both, in this affecting tragedy, was to make an impression on the minds of rational beings every where, and to the end of time. And the impression to be made, was, that God is a holy and righteous God; that while inclined to mercy, he cannot forget the demands of justice, and the danger to his kingdom from the pardon of the guilty; that he must show his feelings on this subject; and show them so clearly and fully, that all his rational creatures shall feel that he honors his law while suspending its operation, as much as he would by the execution of it."†

Dr. Woods, having insisted that much of the language of orthodox writers on this subject is highly figurative, says: "The language, taken literally, would impute a character to God which would excite universal horror. But if understood according to the legitimate principles of interpreting metaphors, it teaches the simple, but all-important truth, that the death of Christ was the means of procuring pardon, or the medium through which salvation is granted."† Well did Dr. Ware rejoin: "Dr. Woods is right in supposing, 'that no objection will lie in the minds of

* Quoted in Unit. Miscellany, vol. v. p. 196.

† Woods' Letters to Unitarians, 1st series, p. 93.

Unitarians,' against the doctrine thus expressed. It is the very manner of expressing the influence of the Atonement, which has been adopted by Unitarian writers."*—Dr. Woods also admits that, "A literal and exact substitution was impossible;"† and yet adds that —"The object of the death of Christ is, to declare, or manifest, that God is righteous, and that in the salvation of sinners he will support the honors of his law, and 'the interests of virtue.'"‡ He afterwards, in words but a single remove for offensiveness from the dramatic language of his brother Professor of Andover, speaks of it as an "*expedient* which the wisdom of God has adopted," to save "the authority of his law."§ We are apt reverently to feel that the Almighty has no need of adopting "expedients," either for the vindication of his righteousness, or for confirming the principles of his moral government.

Accordant as is Dr. Woods' statement first quoted above with the views of Unitarians, Dr. Lyman Beecher's is also quite near them. He says: "That an atonement has been made for sin by Jesus Christ; with reference to which God can maintain the influence of his law and forgive sin, upon condition of repentance towards God and faith in our Lord Jesus Christ; that all men are invited sincerely in this way to return to God, with an assurance of pardon and eternal life if they comply."‖

* Ware's Letters to Trinitarians, 1st series, p. 86.
† As above, p. 101. ‡ p. 102.
§ Woods' Letters as above, pp. 102–3.
‖ Sermon at Worcester, Mass., at ordination of Mr. Hoadly, p. 4.

In this connection take some of the statements of th- Reformers and the older divines. Luther says: "Christ, according to the (Mosaic) law, ought to be hanged, for he sustained the person of a sinner and of a thief, not of one, but of all sinners and thieves." Again: "All the prophets did foresee in spirit that Christ should become the greatest transgressor, murderer, thief, rebel and blasphemer, that ever was or could be in all the world." Still more, he supposes God to say to Christ: "Be thou the person which hath committed the sins of all men; see, therefore, that thou pay and satisfy for them."* Calvin, however, says: "If it be asked how Christ hath done away our sins, and taken away the strife between us and God, and purchased such righteousness as might make Him favorable and well-disposed towards us; it may be in general answered that he hath brought it to pass *by the whole course* of his obedience." Yet he does not hesitate to declare that "in his soul Christ suffered the torments of a damned and forsaken man." "It was requisite, also," he adds, "that he should feel the severity of the divine vengeance, in order to *appease the wrath of God*, and satisfy his justice. Hence it was necessary for him to contend with the powers of hell and eternal death." He speaks, nevertheless, of God's "*appeasing Himself* through the blood of the Cross," while he says that "the burden of damnation, from which we were delivered, was laid upon Christ."† Richard Baxter says: "Christ did give his satisfaction directly and strictly, not to man,

* As quoted by Rd. Wright, *Anti-Satisfactionist*, p. 26.

† Institutes. B. 2, ch. 16, § 5 and § 10; ch. 15, § 4 and § 6.

for whom he suffered, but to God whom he satisfied." And: "Christ's death is a sufficient price and satisfaction to God for the sins of all mankind."* So Bishop Beveridge, referring to the death of Christ, says: "I believe it was not only as much, but infinitely more satisfactory to divine justice, than though I should have died to eternity; for by that means justice is actually and perfectly satisfied already."† President Edwards says that by the death of Christ "all was finished *that was required* in order to satisfy the threatenings of the law, and all *that was necessary* in order to satisfy divine justice." Doubtless, if any thing was required, if any thing was necessary for the one or the other purpose. But he adds: "Then the utmost that *vindictive* justice demanded, even the *whole debt* was paid."‡ That is quite another thing; for we deny that there is any such thing as *vindictive* justice in God's nature or government. Finally, notorious as it is that the pious Watts long before his death would have been glad to alter many of his Hymns had he retained the copyright, those Hymns are to be taken, not only as expressing their author's views when he wrote them, but those of the churches which continue to use them. There we read:

"Well, the Redeemer's gone
  To appear before our God,
To sprinkle o'er the flaming throne,
  With his atoning blood.
Once 'twas a seat of dreadful wrath,
  And shot devouring flame;

* Universal Redemption, pp. 50, § 60.
† Thoughts, p. 44. ‡ Hist. of Redemption, p. 198.

Our God appear'd consuming fire,
And vengeance was his name.
Rich were the drops of Jesus' blood
That calm'd His frowning face,
That sprinkled o'er the burning throne,
And turn'd the wrath to grace."

I need not, I trust, remark upon the horrible picture which such language gives of that all-blessed Being whom our Lord reveals as the FATHER; but surely, in view of the vast variety of statements upon this subject by different minds, we may reasonably ask, yes, quite as pertinently as in regard to the Trinity—which of all is the true statement? Which of all, *par excellence*, is *the* orthodox statement? And, since it is an "essential" point of which we inquire—which of all the self-styled orthodox doctors or churches, is authorized to give us full assurance of what is the absolute truth regarding it?

The history of the doctrine of the Atonement in the Christian Church shows plainly three distinct periods in its developments, each with its *prevailing*, and therefore for the time, *orthodox* theory.* In the first, extending to the eleventh century, the prominent or leading idea is warlike. There was a conflict between the great principles of good and evil, and Christ's death was held to have been the ransom paid to the devil for man's redemption. To be sure the death of Christ was

* I had in mind here the anecdote of the Quaker preacher in London. "Friends," said he, "I have been thinking of a definition of the word *Orthodox*." After a pause he stated it to be—"*Uppermost*." Will any doubt the justness of the definition, when he thinks of what is Orthodoxy at Rome, at St. Petersburgh, at London, at New-York?

also represented as an actual victory over the devil; and Origen even talks of the devil being outwitted.* In the second period, thence to the Reformation, the leading idea is legal. The sinner owes a debt to God, and Christ paid it. In the third, thenceforth to our day, the leading idea is governmental. There could be no forgiveness of sin consistently with the honor and integrity of the Divine Government, except by the amplest vindication of God's violated authority. There must be, at least, such a display of God's indignation against, or abhorrence of sin as the breach of His law, as will prevent the fatal consequences which might otherwise ensue. Christ vindicated God's authority, he made the required display of the divine displeasure by dying on the Cross. To each and all of these theories one great idea is common—satisfaction. In the first the claims of the devil are discharged. In the second, the rights and honor of God are maintained. In the third, the order of God's universe, and the integrity of His moral government, saved and secured.

Or we may take another view of the matter, and find four various schemes, which are or have been held by the orthodox upon the nature of the atonement. The first is specifically that of Satisfaction. By the sacrifices, sufferings, and death of our Lord, he satisfied the justice, while he appeased the wrath of God. He gave his own blood as the great price of our reconciliation to the Father, and discharged the infinite debt in which the race was involved by sin. The second is

* Hagenbach's Hist. of Doctr. i. 189.

that of Substitution. Christ, according to this view, suffered as the substitute for, in the place of sinners, taking upon himself the whole burden of the suffering due them; and thus his sufferings and death were the penalty he literally endured, by as literally taking upon himself the sins of the whole world. Analyse these two schemes carefully, and they are seen to be essentially but one. The third is that of Exhibition. According to this, God, in the sufferings and death of his Son, manifests his hatred of sin, his love of holiness, his regard for the integrity of his Government. There is the fourth, which has been and probably still is held by many Unitarians, according to which the death of Christ is a means—not, indeed, defined—employed in the good pleasure and wisdom of God to bring sinners into that state of freedom and deliverance from sin, which will at the same time make it consistent with Perfect Justice and Holiness to forgive and save them.

Now, we at once object to the first of these schemes, that if the debt has been satisfied and paid, no place is left for God's mercy to act. To talk of mercy in forgiving, or cancelling a debt, which does not exist a moment after it is paid and discharged, is simply absurd. To the second, that to make the innocent suffer in the place or stead of the guilty, is contrary to, impugns, the Divine Justice. It is idle to allege, that we cannot understand the Justice of God, since Justice is and must be ever the same in its nature, be it predicated of God, or of man, His creature and child. By no such allegation can any such mere hypothesis be maintained, especially at the risk of conflict between any of the essential attributes of the All-perfect One. To the third scheme, we object that it is the merest shadow or sham, and seems too much like trifling with a most serious subject. Of the fourth—that which makes the death of Christ an undefined means of our salvation—I have now only to say, that it well avoids the positive errors of the others, and may be all that a man is able satisfactorily to learn from the Scripture on this subject. It is, moreover, so much more rational, so much more in accordance with the general tenor of Scripture, so harmonious with all our conceptions of God derived thence, that its influence on the heart and the life of the believer, must be good. It has beyond doubt a broad basis of truth, on which to stand; and need not be unlearned, even if we are able to press on to clearer and more definite views.

As I approach the examination of the Scripture argument, I rejoice to acknowledge, that the field of controversy on this great subject has, of late years, been narrowed by orthodox concessions and admissions. It was once common in orthodox books and pulpits, to say, that Christ died to appease God's anger—to deliver the sinner from his vengeance—to quench his wrath—to change his wrath into grace—to strip the throne of Heaven of its terrors:—and to insist that his death was the *only* way possible, even to God, for the pardon of human sin, and to secure man's salvation. But now it is widely conceded, that such language is to be understood metaphorically, since as Dr. Woods admits: "Taken literally, it would impute a character to God which would excite universal horror."* The

* Lett. to Unitarians, 1st Ser. p. 86, etc. See also Dwight's Theol vol. ii. p. 412.

same, it is largely agreed, must be said of all those Scriptural expressions, which attribute fierce anger, indignation, wrath, vengeance, to God; or which speak of ransom, redemption, purchase, in reference to Christ's sufferings and death. Archbishop Magee denies, that it is any part of the doctrine of the Church of England, "that men *could not* have been forgiven, unless Christ had suffered to purchase their forgiveness"; and argues at length, that the only *necessity* in the case was "a *moral* necessity, or in other words, a *fitness* and propriety."* The profound Bishop Butler evidently held a similar view.† In like manner I understand a writer in the *New-Englander*, when he says: "Whether this *necessity* consists in the indispensableness of his (Christ's) death as a means of ransoming mankind from Satan, or of appeasing divine anger, or of maintaining the authority of the Law-giver, while the penitent is pardoned, *or in some other principle*, orthodoxy requires *only* that we should believe in the necessity, and ascribe to Christ's death our salvation and the glory of it." He had just before said: "All that is essential to orthodoxy, in respect to the vital doctrine of atonement, is that we should ascribe the salvation of man to *something* which Christ has accomplished by his incarnation and sufferings, and without which salvation would be impossible"; and he adds: "It is *the doctrine*, and *not philosophical explanations*, in which our faith is to be reposed."‡ Precisely; but still it remains true, and causes our chief quarrel with orthodoxy on this great

* On the Atonement, vol. i. p. 143, etc.

† Analogy, part ii. chap. v. p, 262, note, New-York ed. 1843.

‡ *New-Englander*, vol. iii. p. 561.

topic, that in general it insists, in one or another form of statement, upon an absolute necessity on the part of God, that Christ should have suffered and died, before He could forgive and save us; in one or another form of statement, upon what is known as the "governmental" scheme or theory; and therefore sift and analyse it as you may, it still, logically and inevitably, though directly in the face of all Scripture, as I hope to make plain, insists upon the efficacy of Christ's death with or upon God, and not with or upon man. Hence we still read such language as this: "Man (as a sinner) does need to see God undertake for him. In the sufferings and death of Jesus Christ he sees this. . . . There is no place (for him) to flee to, except in this new and strange (!) work of an atoning God. God himself must do something which shall wear the signet of his own high authority. He must step forth from behind the curtains of eternity, and in this world of sin must write somewhere the demonstration of a satisfied law, and a satisfied God. . . . When the sinner sees Jesus Christ undertaking for him, standing in the sinner's own nature, and the sinner's own place, arraigned as his surety, held as his surety, dying as his surety; never giving back till he has met the very last item, and going down into the grave to sanctify and sweeten that last trial-spot of the believer; and when in the opened portals of the tomb, and in the ascension-track of the Redeemer from Olivet to glory, he sees the evidence of *God's* pacification. . . in this new and strange work of God, he finds some foothold for conscience to stand upon. It is just this: Christ has become accountable for him; Christ has met the blow prepared for his head; Christ has died for him; *Deity has grappled with death and the devil;* the tomb has owned a conqueror; and away up by the throne of God bursts the exclamations of angels, 'Lift up your heads, O ye gates! even lift them up, ye everlasting doors, and the King of glory shall come in.'"* In such kind of rhetoric will orthodoxy even now indulge, all unscriptural, as it is. Unitarians feel that here, then, is the vital, cardinal point; that on this alleged necessity really turns the controversy. They feel, that Scripture must be abandoned or ignored, if the orthodox view in this respect be received.

Still the appeal to actual observation of the pulpit would show on the whole a vast change, or modification at least, of the views and statements of orthodox preachers of our day as compared with the days of the New-England Fathers; or indeed, of the divines who either in New-England or New-York were eminent only fifty years ago. Most pertinently does Dr. Ellis ask—"Would Cotton, Hooker, Shepherd, Edwards, or Hopkins have admitted with Dr. E. Beecher, that the system of Orthodoxy is utterly inconsistent with the principles of honor and justice in the Divine government? Or with Professor Park, that the rhetoric of Orthodoxy needs to be torn down, if one would harmonize it with logical truth? Or with Dr. Bushnell, that the death of Christ is a dramatic scene, in which we must discriminate between the subjective and the objective meaning? Ask the aged persons among us who used to listen to Orthodox

* Biblical Repository for October, 1846, pp. 576, 579.

preaching, if its tone, and even its substance, are not changed."* And, we may add, is it as common as once to say, as Dr. Woods did in his Letters to Unitarians, "that we must rely upon Christ's atoning blood, as the *sole ground* of forgiveness?" Is it not getting to be more common to recognize the life, the example, the teachings, the resurrection of our Lord, as part and parcel of his redeeming work?

Not only, then, has the controversy as between Orthodoxy and Unitarianism as to the Atonement been much narrowed, but there is a broad platform of universal consent, on which all believers in the Gospel of the Lord Jesus Christ can stand together. Among them all, of every denominational name, there is no dispute as to his Divine mission, office, and authority; no question whether he be the divinely-appointed mediator between God and man; whether man as a sinner needed such an interposition; whether Christ's sufferings and cross were endured for our salvation; whether Christ died for our sins according to the Scriptures; whether there be any other name under heaven given whereby we must be saved; whether he be not an all-sufficient Saviour, able to save to the uttermost them that come unto God by him. On all these and many other points, the entire Christian world, Romanist, Greek, Protestant, Trinitarian, and Unitarian, is, and always was agreed.

And when we think only of the Protestant portion of Christendom, with very few and insignificant ex-

* Half-Century of the Unitarian Controversy, by Rev. Geo. E. Ellis, D.D., p. 162.

ceptions there is universal agreement that upon the present point of dispute, nay, upon every point of Christian doctrine, the ultimate appeal is, not to decrees of Councils or Synods, not to creeds of man's device of however high antiquity, but to the Scriptures only, the recorded teachings of Christ and his Apostles.

Before, however, going to the Scriptures in the present argument, it seems proper briefly to advert to the subject of Sacrifice; especially under the Old Testament economy.

And in the first place, sacrifices are clearly, I think, of human origin. At least, I can find no evidence that they had at first Divine appointment, or were indeed anything more than natural expressions of the human heart; self-imposed offerings to the deity worshipped, in order to avert his anger or propitiate his favor. Those of the Mosaic religion were purely and exactly ritual; and they were neither expiatory of sin, nor substitutes for punishment, excepting in a civil or political sense. They were symbolical as acts of faith and worship; expressive, as the case might be, either of confession, or supplication, or thanksgiving. Obviously, too, their whole value in the sight of God, their whole efficacy as regarded the worshipper, depended entirely upon the temper of mind or heart in which the offering was made. Let any reader of the Scriptures turn to the first chapter of the prophet Isaiah, and read from the eleventh to the eighteenth verses inclusive, and he will have ample confirmation of this last position.

I must defer the Scriptural argument to another

Lecture. In some sense, all Christian believers hold to the doctrine of Atonement, to the fact of Atonement by Christ. "Now once in the end of the world Christ appeared, to put away sin by the sacrifice of himself."* This none deny. This, of course, Unitarians do not deny. It is not, then, the doctrine, but the statements of the doctrine, and the explanations of the doctrine upon which the Orthodox insist, from which we dissent. Indeed we may take the fact of the efficacy of Christ's sacrifice, as many do, without being able or even attempting to explain it. "How, and in *what* particular way," says Butler†—and few more acute and profound as well as candid and liberal minds ever existed than that great Bishop —"it had this efficacy, there are not wanting persons who have endeavored to explain; but I do not find that the Scripture has explained it. . . . . And if the Scripture has, as surely it has, left this matter of the satisfaction of Christ mysterious, left somewhat in it unrevealed, all conjectures about it must be, if not evidently absurd, yet at least uncertain. Nor has any one reason to complain for want of further information, unless he can show his claim to it."

But holding to the Atonement as we find it in the Scriptures, and hearing on all sides from the Orthodox the persistent assertion of the indispensableness of faith in it as they hold and expound it, I cannot close without a word more, and that of caution. On the most orthodox showing, the Atonement of Christ, notwithstanding all that is said of Salvation by Faith, is

* Heb. 9 : 26. † Analogy, pt. ii. chap. 5, p. 267.

of no manner of avail, irrespective of personal righteousness of heart and life. Admit human obedience, human goodness to be ever so imperfect. Count "good works"—those "good works," which Christ and his inspired Apostles expressly enjoined and insisted upon, and therefore not only "good" but meritorious, aye, *meritorious* in the sight of God—count them, if you dare, to be the "filthy rags" they have been sometimes styled, and by those who should know better; they are, still, essential things—absolutely, positively essential. They will be found essential, if not before, in that day when the secrets of all hearts shall be revealed, as surely as Scripture records the word of God and is therefore true.

LECTURE IX.

ATONEMENT—CONCLUDED.

THE great question, then, upon this subject, as between the orthodox and ourselves, is this: Is the popular doctrine of the Atonement, whether in the form of satisfaction, or exhibition, or any other in which it is stated—for, anomalous as it may seem, this *essential* doctrine is held in so many and such various forms, as to leave the inquirer entirely in the dark as to which is preëminently *the* orthodox, the orthodox of the orthodox form—is it Scripturally true? Unitarianism answers by a positive denial. Such, it declares, is not the doctrine of Scripture. On the contrary, the entire doctrine as thus variously held by the orthodox, in just its peculiarities, or where it differs from the Unitarian view, is based on a misuse or false interpretation of Scripture. In the first place, as we have seen, distinguished orthodox writers agree with us that the whole class of words like ransom, redeem, purchase, is used in the Scripture, in the New Testament especially, in a figurative sense, and is to be so interpreted. Again, as is also admitted by some of our modern opponents, the word "wrath," i. e. of God, is to be understood and interpreted on the same principle. Thus understood, the Scriptures do not by one solitary instance warrant the monstrous idea, that Christ died to appease the wrath of God in any sense. Only a single text even looks like it, namely: "We shall be saved from wrath through him."* But this is not to be understood as though it were literally the wrath of God, like the angry and revengeful passion of man, in very deed enkindled and ready to fall upon the sinner, from which we shall be saved; but rather from the consequences of unrepented sin, the divine judgments upon the wicked and impenitent. Again in our English version, Christ is said in one place to have been set forth as "a propitiation";† but in another,‡ the same word is rendered "mercy-seat," as it should have been in the first.§ Christ, in whom God manifested himself and declared his gracious will, is to us the "mercy-seat"; as that of old in the Jewish worship was the place of God's manifested presence and favor to Israel. But in two other places where the English word "propitiation" occurs,‖ it is a different word in the original, and should have been rendered "propitiatory sacrifice." Christ in a somewhat loose sense, was such a sacrifice—but the sacrifice was made for our sakes, to reconcile us to God, not God to us. The object could not be to reconcile Him or render Him propitious or merciful; for both of these He always was, and, from His essential nature as the Father All-Perfect, must be; but to quicken our repent-

* Rom. 5 : 9. Vid. Robinson's Lex. of N. T. verb. Ὀργή. Schleusner, ibid.—Archbishop Newcome renders the word in his text *anger;* but in his note explains—"We shall be finally saved through him from *punishment.*"

† Rom. 3 : 25. ‡ Heb. 9 : 5.

§ Bishop Marsh, Ernesti, Adam Clark, so render it in Rom. 3 : 25; and Dr. Wardlaw prefers this rendering. See for illustration, Exodus 25 : 17–23. ‖ 1 John 2 : 2; 4 : 10.

ance and obedience, by assuring us of the certainty of the divine forgiveness. "It appears to me most probable," says Dr. Carpenter, "that when the Apostle says that Jesus was a propitiation or reconciliation concerning our sins, he refers to *all* which Jesus did and suffered in order to render men fit objects for the divine mercy."* Again: never is it said or countenanced in the Scriptures, that any thing which Christ did or suffered, caused or excited the grace or favor, or mercy of God; though in great variety and amount of expression, they assure us that Christ's coming, and suffering, and dying, was all of God's free grace, of His great love and kindness towards us.† Never is it said that God is, or was to be, reconciled to us, as has been and is the too common representation in orthodox pulpits and writings; but always that we are reconciled to Him, by Jesus Christ.‡ Yet once more Christ is said to have "died for us," "suffered for us";§ but how manifestly as the chief expression of the love of God to our race, or as an example of holy disinterestedness and self-sacrifice! "God commendeth His love towards us, in that, while we were yet sinners, Christ died for us." "Christ also suffered for us, leaving us an example, that ye should follow his steps." Such is the teaching of the Apostles of our Lord. When we consider his history and his fate; coming forth as a Reformer and a Saviour; with the highest credentials, claiming uncompromisingly to have direct

* Unitarianism the Doctrine of the Gospel, p. 378.

† E. g. Rom. 3 : 24, 25 ; 5 : 15–21 ; Ephes. 2 : 4–10 ; John 4 : 9, 10.

‡ Rom. 5 : 10 ; 11 : 15 ; 2 Cor. 5 : 18, 19, 20 ; Col. 1 : 19–21.

§ Rom. 5 : 6–8 ; 1 Pet. 2 : 21 ; 3 : 17, 18 ; 4 : 1.

divine authority as specially sent of God; devoting himself from first to last to the great work of his mission and ministry; sparing himself no labor or suffering; addressing men grossly corrupt, "dead in trespasses and sins," in the tenderest and most earnest terms, that he might awaken and save them; exercising his miraculous power in offices of love and mercy; yet constantly opposed with the most subtle malice, cavilled at, persecuted, arrested, subjected to a mock trial, and then condemned and put to a cruel and ignominious death; what confirmation of the Apostles' words is here! What illustration of their position, that he suffered and died for us!

I am now led to consider somewhat specially the Epistle to the Hebrews, since a great part of the difficulty, I am persuaded, existing in the popular mind upon this subject, grows out of the peculiar character and language of this Epistle. I enter into no critical inquiry as to the authorship of the Epistle, that *questio vexata* ever since the second century; for I take it as it stands — if not written by St. Paul — as still a canonical book, of apostolic origin and authority; and shall use and treat it accordingly.

What, then, is the object or design of this Epistle?

The first portion, extending to the nineteenth verse of the tenth chapter, is doctrinal. First, the writer asserts the preëminence of Christ over all the former prophets and messengers of God; and thence argues for the superiority of his dispensation over all that preceded it. Next, in the third chapter, he argues for his superiority specifically over Moses; and for the superiority of that spiritual "rest" which he ensures to his followers, over the Israelitish "rest" in Canaan.

Then, from the fourth to the seventh chapters inclusive, he sets forth Christ's priesthood and its superiority to the Levitical priesthood; and thence infers the speedy and entire abolition of the Jewish ceremonial law. Again, to the nineteenth verse of the tenth chapter, he earnestly endeavors to reconcile the Hebrew converts or the Hebrew inquirers to the offensive doctrine of a crucified Messiah, that great "stumbling-block" and "rock of offence" to the Hebrew mind; by representing Christ's death, even on the Cross, as a sacrifice of vastly superior efficacy and worth to any or all under the Old Dispensation, and which they but foreshadowed.—The remainder of the Epistle is simply practical.

It is not at all strange, when one examines, too, the language of the Epistle, that the chief arguments for the expiatory sacrifice of Christ in the Atonement should be thence drawn. And yet, all the language which at first sight seemingly supports, or is alleged to support that dogma, is easily explained by reference to the design, circumstances, position of the writer. He was a Hebrew addressing Hebrews. He was, as is most evident, profoundly versed in Hebrew lore, modes of thought, association of ideas, as well as its history and ritual. He not unnaturally, therefore, employs the *argumentum ad hominem*;* an argument which, though

* "A third way is to press a man with consequences drawn from his own principles or concessions. This is known under the name of *argumentum ad hominem*."—Locke on the Understanding, ii. 238.

"The *argumentum ad hominem* consists in appealing to a man's acts, or previous declarations, *or avowed principles*, as being inconsistent with the position he is at present maintaining."—Wilson's Logic, p. 336.

not absolutely of conclusive force, is yet sometimes of great rhetorical efficiency; and which, while of special aptness for his purpose, he uses with the utmost possible skill. But though it was a good argument to the Hebrews of that day, it by no means follows that it is to us.—This view accounts also for the remarkable fact, that in none of the Epistles of which St. Paul is the universally accredited writer, in no other Epistle, indeed, of the New Testament, is there the least allusion to the priestly office or the High Priesthood of Christ; but in this it is made prominent. To the Hebrew mind it was a conception at once striking and forcible.

It is, moreover, to be remarked in this connection, that in only two instances in *his* Epistles, throwing this Epistle aside, does St. Paul speak of Christ's death as an offering or a sacrifice; while in no other Epistle of any Apostle, except this to the Hebrews, is it ever so spoken of. The two instances referred to occur, the first in the first Epistle to the Corinthians,* and thus reads: "For even Christ our Passover is sacrificed for us." Now, it is perfectly well understood by any ordinary reader of the Old Testament, that the Paschal Lamb, the Lamb of the Passover, slain at that great Feast, was in no sense a sacrifice; it was simply the symbol of the ancient deliverance of the ancestral Hebrew race when the destroying angel *passed over*, i. e. spared their homes, on his mission of death to the first-born of the Egyptians. Slain at the Passover season as Christ was, his death, though no more sacrificial than that of the Paschal Lamb, marked a far higher

* 5: 7.

spiritual deliverance, and so warranted the Apostle's beautiful figure. The other passage is in the Epistle to the Ephesians, and thus reads: "Christ also hath loved us, and hath given himself for us, an offering and a sacrifice to God, for a sweet-smelling savor."* But in what sense the Apostle here used this language, and that he certainly did not intend by it to represent the death of his Lord as literally an expiatory sacrifice, may be seen by reference to his Epistle to the Philippians; where, in the original Greek, in both passages, he uses the identical *word* alike and correctly rendered in both by our translators "sacrifice"; and in both, the identical *phrase* which they have rendered in the former "a sweet-smelling savor," and in the latter—as synonymous with it—"an odor of a sweet smell;" a phrase certainly expressive rather of an eucharistic, free-will, or thank-offering, than of a piacular or expiatory one.†

* Ephes. 5 : 2 : "Christ, from good-will to men, made a sacrifice of his life upon the Cross; and his benevolent and disinterested conduct in this instance was highly acceptable to God, which is here expressed by the sacrificial term, 'an offering of fragrant odor.'"—Belsham's Ep. of St. Paul, h. l. iii. 253, note. "Usteri (St. Paul's System, 4th ed., p. 113) expresses himself upon our passage as follows: 'The context contains only this: Christ has, in his yielding up of himself, so well-pleasing to God, left us a pattern. That is to say, the giving up himself by Christ was, as we know from Phil. 2 : 8, at the same time an act of obedience towards God, and therefore attended by the Divine approval. *'Οσμὴ εὐωδίας* at Phil. 4 : 18, and *εὐωδία* at 2 Cor. 2 : 15, are used in a similar way to denote the Divine well-pleasedness, *without the slightest allusion being made to an Atonement.*'"—Olshausen, Comm. in h. l. v. 123.

† Philip. 4 : 18 : "We see how familiar to the Jews were the rites of their religion, and how they supplied them with a constant source of

When, therefore, we find the writer to the Hebrews especially laboring this point, we infer that he was grappling with Jewish difficulties, and intent on overcoming them. On candid Jewish minds his views and arguments, and the language in which they were couched, were fitted to make, and doubtless did make a vivid and deep impression. No more doubt can there justly be, however, than that strong as at times seems his language, quoted as it so often is in an isolated way, he never meant to teach that the bloody sacrifices of the Mosaic ritual of themselves actually atoned for or removed the guilt of sin. When, therefore, he says in one passage—"without shedding of blood there is no remission,"* he simply states a fact in the Mosaic economy, namely, that no *ritual* offences were remitted except by the "shedding of blood" in the prescribed sacrifice. "This leads him to remark," says Dr. Carpenter, "that there was a peculiar fitness that, in the new dispensation, purification should be made with superior sacrifices. What he refers to obviously was the death of Christ; and he remarks (v 26) that the Christ 'hath been manifested for the removal of sin,'† to give every suitable aid and en-

figures of speech. If a present of money was called *a sacrifice well-pleasing to God*, can we be surprised that so heroical an act of virtue as that which Christ manifested in his death should also be called *a sacrifice well-pleasing to God?* . . . . And yet, the death of Christ has been considered so much a sacrifice, as by this means alone the anger of God against sin has been appeased, and that by this means only he has become propitious to offending sinners."—Priestley, Notes on N. T. h. l.

* 9 : 22.

† In the Received Version—"hath appeared, to put away sin."

couragement in the acquisition of holiness in heart and life, 'by the sacrifice of himself.'"* Thus interpreting him, we learn how to reconcile the declaration—"without shedding of blood there is no remission"—with what had been said before, and what he says afterwards. Before, he had said that the "gifts and sacrifices" of "the first covenant," "while as the first tabernacle was yet standing," "could not make him that did the service perfect *as pertaining to the conscience*"; and again: "If the blood of bulls and of goats, and the ashes of an heifer sprinkling the unclean, sanctifieth *to the purifying of the flesh*," that is, from *ritual* impurity; how much more shall the blood of Christ, who, through the eternal Spirit offered himself without spot to God, *purge your conscience from dead works* to serve the living God!"† Afterwards, too, he emphatically says: "It is not *possible* that the blood of bulls and of goats *should take away sins*."‡ What could more clearly prove the *symbolical* character and *mere ritual* efficacy of the bloody sacrifices of the old dispensation; and, therefore, the transcendent *moral* purpose and character, and paramount *spiritual* efficacy of the sacrifice of Christ? Besides, be it remembered in confirmation of the ground that the death of Christ was not, could not be, literally, an expiatory sacrifice,—that, as we saw above, he is our "High Priest." That the same person should be at once and literally high priest, and victim, is to confound all distinctions of terms and of things, to state a contradiction and an impossibility. Nay, if we look carefully into the

* Unitarianism, etc. p. 386.

† Hebr. 9: 1, 8, 9, 13, 14.

‡ Ibid. 10: 4.

Scriptures, we shall find that Christ is not only a "priest" and a "High Priest" and a "sacrifice," but he is "the Lamb slain," yes, and "slain from the foundation of the world"; he is a "door," a "way," a "vine," a "chief corner-stone"; a "captain," a "king," a "shepherd"; "the Lion of the tribe of Juda, the Root of David." Is he, then, could he be, literally all these? Must it not in every case be metaphorically, or at most, by way of accommodation to the various offices and relations in which he is revealed, and which he sustains?

It has been so common with the orthodox to charge us with placing no reliance on the death of Christ, or ascribing to it no efficacy in the salvation of man, that some may be surprised to hear me give the charge a flat denial. No Christian Unitarian has any doubt of the value and importance of that event, or of the reality of the sacrifice therein embodied. The dispute does not turn on the point whether Christ "died for the ungodly," "died for our sins," "died for all," for these are but the simple declarations of that Scripture on which we claim to stand; but, upon the interpretation of the special effects, the peculiar virtue, the reach of the influence of his death. And, though differences exist among us as to these points, they do not affect our general faith, nor are they in themselves so great as those which obtain among our opponents.

Let it be understood, then, that among Unitarians, there are three prevalent opinions upon the effects of the death of the Saviour. The first, simply affirms the fact that the death of Christ was *a* means of pardon, without determining either the nature, mode of operation, or exact extent of influence as regards the Deity; it regards it, in the words of Mr. Sparks, as "a sacrifice designed to expiate, or take away the guilt of sin, by its influence in procuring the pardon of God, which would not have been granted without such a sacrifice." This view closely resembles that of Bishop Butler, Dr. Samuel Clarke, and Archbishop Magee* of the English Church, and was held by Socinus and the Polish Unitarians in general; by Drs. Price and John Taylor, and many English Unitarians of their day; it is the faith of the Genevan and other Swiss Unitarians of our own time. The second opinion, embraces reasons why God accepts the death of Christ as a means of pardon, namely, on account of his holiness and obedience; "for the sufferings and death of Christ, he has been rewarded by the Father, in an exalted state, with supreme power to forgive sins, to make effectual intercession for transgressors, and bestow salvation on all such as are truly penitent and worthy." Some of the early Socinians held this; and it was held by Thomas Emlyn, Henry Taylor, Dr. Benson, and others in England and our own country. The third, views the agency of Christ in the work of salvation as affecting man alone, and not God; "that his death was chiefly instrumental in leading men to embrace his religion, obey his commands, repent of their wickedness, forsake their sins, and attain that perfect holiness of character, which God is always ready to accept and reward with pardon, and without which no man can

* Butler's Analogy, p. 281; Magee on Atonement, i. pp. 18, 19.

be fitted for his future kingdom." This has been always the view of a large portion of those who are and have been known abroad and at home as Unitarians; it was the view of Priestley, and of those in his day who were called in England, Humanitarians; and is the most distinctly antagonistic to the genuine Calvinistic view, which insists that the whole effect is on God.*

Dr. Channing says: "We have no desire to conceal the fact, that a difference of opinion exists among us, in regard to an interesting part of Christ's mediation; I mean in regard to the precise influence of his death on our forgiveness. Many suppose, that this event contributes to our pardon, as it was a principal means of confirming his religion and of giving it power over the mind; in other words, that it procures forgiveness by leading to that repentance and virtue, which is the great and only condition on which forgiveness is bestowed. Many of us are dissatisfied with this explanation, and think that the Scriptures ascribe the remission of sins to Christ's death, with an emphasis so peculiar, that we ought to consider this event as having a special influence in removing punishment, though the Scriptures may not reveal the way in which it contributes to this end."† Dr. Henry Ware, Sen., says: "He (Christ) was our redeemer, by doing and suffering all that was necessary to effect our deliverance from the power of sin, to bring us to repentance and holiness, and thus make us the fit object of forgiveness

* Sparks' Lett. to Miller, p. 199; whose words, as will be seen, I have quoted above.

† Works, iii. pp. 88, 89.

and the favor of heaven."* Dr. G. E. Ellis says: "Orthodoxy, not through warrant of any thing which Unitarianism proclaims, but by one of the unkind arts of controversy, attempts to confine our construction of the atoning death of Christ to the power and service of an example. We protest against the charge; we repel it. What some Unitarians may have recognized as a subsidiary and incidental lesson from the cross of Christ, ought not to be thus represented as exhausting our view of it. It is not our doctrine that the death of Christ becomes efficacious to us as an example, or even that it is especially needed or available in that direction. Christ is to us a victim, a sacrifice; his death was a sacrificial death. Its method and purpose and influence fix a new, a specific, a peculiar, an eminent meaning to the word *sacrifice*, when used of him. Indeed, the highest and most sacred signification of the word ought forever to be associated with *his* sacrifice. But, in conformity with that deciding distinction . . . of a God-ward or a man-ward intent in the cross, we regard Jesus as a sacrifice *for man*, but not as a sacrifice *to God*. The difference is an infinite one, as indicated by those two prepositions attached respectively to the creature and the Creator. We regard Christ as a victim offered by human sin for human redemption; as one who could not have been our Redeemer but by being 'faithful unto death,' and as a willing sacrifice for our redemption. He was led as a lamb to the slaughter, and his murderers, as the Prophet foretold that they would, had wrongly 'esteemed him stricken, smitten of God, and afflicted.' (Isaiah

* Letters to Trinitarians, p. 92.

53 : 4.) But instead of being 'stricken of God,' he was 'wounded for our iniquities.' 'He tasted death for every man'; not *eternal* death, but death. He was nailed to the cross to secure our salvation, but not to make reparation for our sins to God."*

Where, then, at this stage of the discussion, is the great difference between the Orthodox and ourselves? They say that repentance and reformation are not enough, of themselves and alone, to secure God's forgiveness and acceptance of sinners; that the sufferings and death of Christ were indispensable to the end that God, consistently with the integrity of his moral character and government, should forgive sin. We say, not only that God could, but that He promised by his Prophets and by Christ himself that He would—nay, that He always did and always will, forgive sin on repentance and amendment of life; and that the sufferings and death of Christ were necessary, as essential parts of his mediatorial work, the more effectually to lead men to repentance and holy living, and thus prove them to be reconciled to God, as the Divine conditions of pardon. You may gather illustrations of the first branch of this position, from all parts of the Old Testament. Jehovah proclaimed himself to Moses, as the "Lord God, merciful and gracious, ... forgiving iniquity and transgression and sin." When Moses intercedes with Jehovah for the people, he refers to this very proclamation, and on the strength of it says: "'Pardon, I beseech thee, the iniquity of this people, according unto the greatness of thy mercy, and as thou

* Half-Century of the Unitarian Controversy, pp. 193, 194.

hast forgiven this people from Egypt even until now.' And the Lord said, 'I have pardoned according to thy word.'" Isaiah also declares: "Let the wicked forsake his way, and the unrighteous man his thoughts; and let him return unto the Lord, and He will have mercy upon him; and to our God, and He will abundantly pardon."* Surely the New Testament is not behind the Old in this matter. Neither John the Baptist, nor our Lord, intimated any conditions beyond Repentance, and its corresponding fruits in the life, as the preparation for receiving the Gospel and being accepted of God; and how fully and broadly, not to add how beautifully and tenderly, did the latter teach this efficacy of Repentance in the exquisite parable of the Prodigal! Accordingly, when our Lord had ascended to the Father, St. Paul "taught publicly, and from house to house, testifying both to the Jews, and also to the Greeks, Repentance toward God, and Faith toward our Lord Jesus Christ"; while the beloved disciple declares: "If we confess our sins, God is faithful and just"—not simply gracious and merciful—but "faithful," as if in recognition of his ancient promises and dealings, and "just," as if all conditions of pardon had been met—"faithful and just to forgive us our sins, and to cleanse us from all iniquity."†

Again, while both parties agree that the essence of the Atonement as to its purpose and result is Reconciliation, the Orthodox insist that its effect is on God, and

* Exod. 34 : 6, 7 ; Numb. 14 : 17–19 ; Isa. 55 : 7 ; see also Ezek. 18, throughout, and that glorious 103d Psalm.

† Matt. 3 : 2, 8 ; 4 : 17 ; Luke 15 ; Acts 20 : 20, 21 ; 1 John 1 : 9 ; see also Luke 24 : 46, 47.

we hold that it is on man. And here it is to be remarked that this English word *Atonement*, which is so constantly repeated in orthodox pulpits, occurs only once in the whole of our English version;* and should there, beyond all question, read *Reconciliation*, as indeed it does in the margin of the Polyglott. Besides, the Greek noun *καταλλαγη*, there rendered "Atonement," is, in the only two other texts in which it occurs in the original, rendered "Reconciliation";† and in the verse preceding that in which it is rendered "Atonement," and elsewhere in St. Paul's Epistles, those words which are rendered "reconciled," "reconcile," "reconciling," are all from the same Greek root.‡ To recur, then, to our respective positions, who were the parties at variance? The answer on all sides is, God and man. Which was to be reconciled? The Orthodox, as I have said, always insist that God was to be reconciled to man; and we, with the New Testament for our warrant, which, without a solitary exception uniformly so declares, that man was to be reconciled to God. I repeat, and I beg especial attention to

* Rom. 5: 11. † 2 Cor. 5: 18 and 19.

‡ Rom. 5: 9; Ephes. 2: 16; Col. 1: 20, 21.—It is well known that at the time our English version was made, the word Atonement, i. e. At-one-ment, was synonymous with, or literally signified Reconciliation; and is so used by the writers of that period. Our translators, doubtless, so used it. Examples in cotemporary writers are frequent. Here are two from Shakspeare:

"He and Aufidius can no more *atone*
Than violentest contrariety."
Coriolanus, Act. iv. sc. 6.

"He seeks to make *atonement*
Between the Duke of Gloster and your brothers."
Richard III., Act. i. sc. 3.

the fact, that there is not the least Scriptural authority for speaking of the sufferings and death of Christ, as either intended or adapted for that most unnecessary and gratuitous work of reconciling God to man. On the contrary, St. Paul expressly says: "When we were enemies, we were reconciled to God by the death of His Son."—"All things are of God, who hath reconciled us to Himself by Jesus Christ."—"God was in Christ reconciling the world unto Himself"—"that he might reconcile both (Jews and Gentiles) unto God in one body by the Cross."—"It pleased the Father that in him (Christ) should all fulness dwell; and having made peace by the blood of his Cross, by him to reconcile all things unto Himself; . . . . and you, that were sometimes alienated, and enemies in your mind by wicked works, yet now hath he reconciled." St. Peter also says: "Christ hath once suffered for sins, the just for the unjust, that he might bring us to God."* Surely, no language could be more explicit.

Once more; all sections of the Church agree, first, in the necessity of removing the guilt of sin and its consequences, before man can be a truly happy being here or hereafter. Secondly, that the present condition of mankind is, in point of fact, in the case of every individual of the race, more or less sinful; "all have sinned;" and the joys of the blessed can only be experienced by the penitent and the holy. Thirdly, that the removal of the consequences of sin is the work of God. Man may avoid and repent of sin, but he cannot of himself remove its consequences. In other words,

* Rom. 5 : 10; 2 Cor. 5 : 18, 19; Ephes. 2 : 16; Col. 1 : 19–21; 1 Peter 3 : 18.

Repentance is our work, Pardon God's. Hence the question, how can we escape the deserved and threatened punishment of our sins and be saved? And all answer, that Pardon and Salvation to every believer are by and through Christ, the appointed Mediator between God and Man.

What, then, at this stage of the discussion, is the matter of debate? Obviously, the mode or means by which Christ saves us. The Orthodox say—by suffering and dying in our stead; for, this notion of vicariousness or substitution, that is, the standing in the place or stead of another, may be found in every modification of their views on this subject almost without exception; and again, they say—by sustaining the honor of God's law, and the integrity of His moral character and government as being perfectly just, righteous and holy, through the literal voluntary expiation which Christ made upon the Cross; thus rendering it at once consistent and safe for God to forgive human sin on the repentance and faith of the sinner. We say, on the contrary, that Christ saves us, so far as his sufferings and death are concerned, through their moral influence and power upon man; the great appeal which they make being not to God, but to the sinner's conscience and heart; thus aiding in the great work of bringing him into reconciliation with, or reconciling him to, his Father in heaven. They "purge the conscience," as the writer to the Hebrews expresses it,* which is precisely the sinner's need. I am glad in passing to remark that this view has of late been ad-

* Heb. 9:14.

mitted and preached by some Orthodox divines ;* and also, that it is not as common as it once was, to speak of satisfying the justice or appeasing the wrath of the Almighty.

But bear in mind, that though we yield to none in our grateful acknowledgments of the vast importance and worth in the work of our salvation of the sufferings, the death, the Cross of Christ, we do not emphasize them to the degree of saying, that they were or are the sole and exclusive means of accomplishing that work. We do not, because the Scriptures authorize no such view. In them we are over and over again said to be saved by many and various other things, besides the Cross, besides the agony and death of our Lord. In that passage in the Epistle to the Romans to which I have before referred, though we are said to be "*reconciled* to God *by the death* of His Son," Paul expressly declares that "we shall be *saved by his life*."† Again, in the same Epistle, "we are saved by Hope" ;‡ while to the Ephesians he says, "by Grace ye are saved."§ In his first Epistle to the Corinthians, it is by what he calls "the foolishness of preaching"; and again, by the "Gospel" which "he preached."‖ Peter, moreover, intimates that we are saved "by the Resurrection of Jesus Christ"; and Paul certainly gives pre eminence to the Resurrection, as though that were the more important. "Christ that died," he says, "yea,

* As by Pres. Wayland, sermon at Hague's Installation, pp. 7 and seq. See also Barnes' Introd. Essay to Butler's Anal. pp. 7 and seq See also Barnes' Essay, Introductory to Butler's Analogy, pp. xxxix. et seq. † 5 : 10. ‡ 8 : 24. § 2 : 5.

‖ 1 Ep. 1 : 21 ; 15 : 2.

rather, that hath *risen again*." Especially does he lay the greater stress on the Resurrection of our Lord in that grand argument in the first Epistle to the Corinthians. "If Christ be *not risen*, then is our preaching vain, and your faith is also vain. Yea; and we are found false witnesses of God, because we have testified of God that He raised up Christ, whom He raised not up, if so be that the dead rise not. For if the dead rise not, Christ is not raised: and"—mark the distinctness of his language—"*if Christ be not raised*, your faith is vain; *ye are yet in your sins!*"* What, in the light of this reasoning of Paul, becomes of the idea that the death of Christ, his sufferings, his Crucifixion, were the sole means by which we are saved? It utterly vanishes; and then rises before us the more just, reasonable, and scriptural view, that we are saved by the whole mediatorial agency in which Christ was engaged from first to last; in which, indeed, he is, and will be, engaged, until "he shall have delivered up the kingdom to God, even the Father."†

This, then, is our position. Salvation is reconciliation to God; and that Reconciliation (At-one-ment) is accomplished by Christ, in "saving us from our sins," in turning away every one of us from his iniquities," which alone alienate us from God.‡ But how? By all that he was and is; all that he taught, did, and is doing; and by all that he suffered for our sake. Not by one, but by all of these.

By his whole life on earth, as our sinless, holy, benevolent Exemplar; by his piety to God; his love to

* 1 Peter 3: 21; Rom. 8: 34; 1 Cor. 15: 14–17. † 1 Cor. 15: 24.
‡ Matt. 1: 23; Acts 3: 26; Col. 1: 21.

man; his works of mercy; his unwearied benevolence even to his persecutors; his patience under wrong and suffering; his perfect obedience and submission to his Father's will.

By his miracles; wrought in attestation of his Divine mission, in proof that he was the Son of God, and that God was with him and in him.

By his instructions; conveyed in the Sermon on the Mount, in his exquisite parables, in his solemn warnings against sin, in his call to repentance, in his encouraging offers and promises to the faithful, in his parting counsels, in all "the gracious words which proceeded out of his mouth."

By his great Revelations of the Fatherhood of God, the parental character of His Government and law, the infinite embrace of His Love and Mercy, and His free and unpurchased grace in Christ; of the Immortality of man, of the vast trust and stewardship of life, of our moral accountableness, and the retributive character of the eternal future.

And, while denying that the Scriptures ever attribute our salvation to the death of Christ alone, we thankfully believe, as prominent in his entire agency for that great end, that God "having made peace by the blood of his Cross," we are saved by the moral influence and power of our Lord's death and sacrifice; a true, real, voluntary sacrifice; not made to God, indeed, for then it would seem that He needed to be propitiated or rendered merciful, when in His own infinite nature He was always and perfectly merciful; but for man, in man's behalf, for man's sake, for man's present and everlasting good. By this view of Christ's sacrifice, can it alone be made to harmonize with God's free forgiveness of sin. "I, even I, am He, saith the Lord, that blotteth out thy transgressions *for mine own sake*," we read in the Old Testament; and in the New, St. Paul speaks of our "being freely justified by his grace through the redemption that is in Christ Jesus."* In this view, it most emphatically appeals to man's conscious sense of obligation, obedience, gratitude, and love to the Saviour, and to the Father who "spared not His own Son, but delivered him up for us all."

Finally, we are saved by our Lord's Resurrection; proving him to be "the Son of God with power"; confirming our faith that we are sharers in his "victory," and that "because he lives, we shall live also"; by his glorious Ascension to the Father, and his present and perpetual Intercession. "By all these means and ways," in the words of Tillotson, which he says "have all a great influence in reforming and saving mankind," Christ "is the author and cause of our salvation."†

To all this it is objected that we take away the last hope of the sinner, the Infinite Atonement of the Saviour made to God; that being the essential pre-requisite to pardon of sin, which is an infinite evil as committed against the Infinite One. But on the highest and most explicit Scriptural authority, we deny that any such Atonement was essential—nay, was made. God could and did, before Christ entered the world, freely pardon sin on repentance, as I have already shown. Besides,

* Isa. 43 : 25; Rom. 3 : 24. † Works, vol. vii. p. 2069.

man is a finite being, and can, therefore, perform no infinite action, good or bad. If, too, sin be infinite, then all sins are equal; there can be no gradations in guilt, since there are none in infinity. Nay, every single sin must then be infinite, and there should be as many infinite atonements as there have been sins committed. The absurdity of this need not surely be shown. If, moreover, our sins, our evil deeds, be infinite because against an Infinite Being, so must be our virtues, our good deeds, which are for Him; and then—as is so often and falsely charged upon us—might we put ourselves on our own merits with a vengeance! If sin, however, be not infinite, as we insist it cannot be, being the act of a finite being like man, then was there no need of that impossible thing, an Infinite Atonement.

But the fact is, that the Trinitarian majority in the church, with all the tenacity in which they hold and teach that an Infinite Atonement was necessary, long ago stultified themselves by the assumption that the Atonement of Christ is of that character, and therefore fully meets the required conditions. Is it so? Is it according to their own statements of the doctrine, Infinite? Notoriously not. "No doubt," says Prof. Tayler Lewis, "it has been the common doctrine of the Church, or the great majority of true Christians in all ages, ... that the Deity is immutable, and therefore, as far as the one implies the other, impassible."* When pressed, then, by the inquiry, 'Did God Himself suffer and die on Calvary?' their reply must be—'Yes—God the Son.'—'*Did* God the Son, then, as God or in his Divine nature, suffer and die on Calva-

* Bibl. Repository, 3d Ser. vol. ii. p. 411.

ry?'—'No—but in his Human nature,' must be the answer. How obvious for us to rejoin—'Then you show no Infinite Atonement. All human nature is finite. You hold that in his human nature, Christ was entirely human; that he had a human body and a human soul. If he suffered and died only in his human nature, only as man, his sufferings and death by no proper use of language can be called infinite, by no possibility can be infinite. No Infinite Atonement is shown.'

If any one will take the trouble to turn to Bishop Pearson's work on the Creed, he will see how the boldest statements in regard to the sufferings of Christ apparently as God "on first view and on repeated reviews"—to use an expression of Prof. Lewis—end in a most lame and impotent conclusion. "That Word which was in the beginning, which then was with God, and was GOD, in the fulness of time being made flesh, did suffer . . . . GOD purchased the Church with *His own blood* . . . . When he (our Saviour) was buffeted and scourged, there was no other person sensible of those pains, than the Eternal Word which before all worlds was *impassible;* when he was crucified and died, there was no other person which gave up the ghost but the Son of Him, and so of *the same nature* with Him, *who only hath immortality.*" But with all this strength of language, he, nevertheless, in the same paragraph asserts, that "the Lord of Glory, and most truly God, took upon him the nature of man, *and in that nature,* being still the same person that before he was, did suffer."* That this was his belief as it is

* Pp. 186, 187

"the prevalent hypothesis" among the orthodox, is even more distinctly stated by him elsewhere. "As we ascribe the Passion to the Son alone, so must we attribute it to that *nature* which is his alone, that is the *human*. . . . . Far be it, therefore, from us, to think that the Deity, which is immutable, could suffer; which only hath immortality, could die." Hence the conclusion after all is, that the human, the finite nature, was all that suffered, was that which died. "Thus," says Channing, "this vaunted system goes out—in words. The Infinite victim proves to be frail man, and God's share in the sacrifice is a mere fiction. I ask with solemnity, Can this doctrine give one moment's ease to the conscience of an unbiassed, thinking man?"*

This grand and fundamental difficulty in the theory which has so long prevailed in the Church, was perceived and deeply felt by the late George G. Griffin, of New-York, a barrister of acknowledged ability and accomplishment. In his work entitled, "The Sufferings of Christ," he boldly and manfully takes and attempts to maintain the position, "That Christ suffered in both his natures." In the course of his argument, he says: "Without adequate suffering not a soul could be saved. The second person of the Trinity voluntarily became the vicarious Sufferer for the redeemed. The substitution was not to depress the awful standard of retributive justice. The Glory of the Godhead was to be maintained; heaven must be satisfied, hell silenced. The substituted coin was to bear the scrutiny of eternity. The redeeming God lacked not

* Works, iii. 18ᵒ

capacity to suffer."* This last sentence is of special significance in the connection; because, as I have said, he maintains, contrary to the old Athanasian, which he calls the now "prevalent theory," or "hypothesis," namely that "God is impassible," or, in other words, that "the Divine nature is incapable of suffering," that the Divine nature can and did suffer in Christ. Hence he speaks of "the incarnate, suffering, dying, risen God." "God, the Son, suffered not by proxy. . . . If the God suffered not in his ethereal essence, the Scriptural declarations of his sufferings are not true, in the amplitude of Scriptural verity. . . . The sufferings, in the delineation of which even Inspiration seems to falter, were not limited to the finite, but pervaded also the most sacred recesses of that infinite essence which went to constitute the holy union, styled by our opponents," (so he calls the orthodox "advocates" of the "popular theory,") "the person of Christ. The sufferings of the man lay within the limits of Scriptural delineation. The agonies of the God none but a God could conceive. Perhaps even Omnipotence could not make them intelligible to creature comprehension."† It is no part of my purpose to undertake specially the refutation of Mr. Griffin; but simply to show to what extraordinary language he was obliged to resort in the statement and unfolding of a theory which should logically meet the demands of Orthodoxy. He saw that "the prevalent theory" of his orthodox "opponents," that only the *finite* human nature of Christ suffered, while an *infinite* atonement was demanded by the alleged

* Second edition, 1846, pp. 48, 50.

† Pp. 49, 82, 88.

necessity of the case, could not be sustained against the Unitarian objections. "If Christendom," he accordingly says, "would extirpate the Unitarian heresy, let a concentrated blow be aimed at the major proposition of its upholding syllogism.* Wrest from it its earth-woven mantle of the divine impassibility. Strip it of its armor of proof. That Christ suffered in his united natures, is a position deeply imbedded in the everlasting truth of Sacred Writ. The hypothesis of God's impassibility, has no foundation in his Holy Word. Divine impassibility is the chief corner-stone of the Unitarian faith. Remove that corner-stone, and the whole structure will totter to its foundation."†

Not so fast, we should be tempted to say to our author, were he living. "Divine impassibility" is *not* "the corner-stone of the Unitarian faith." We recognize with St. Paul no "other foundation than that is laid, which is Jesus Christ"; and we claim, as he elsewhere expresses himself, to have "built upon the foundation of the Apostles and Prophets, JESUS CHRIST himself being the chief CORNER-STONE."‡ But, supposing "Divine impassibility" were, as you allege, "the corner-stone of the Unitarian faith"—who laid it? It *has been and is*, by your own showing, "the prevalent theory" of Christendom, from the time of Athanasius in the fourth century to this. His "brilliant name," you say, joined to the "confident pretensions" of his "bold hypothesis," "seems, for near fifteen centuries, to have dazzled the mental vision of the wisest

* Namely, "it is not 'fitting to God' to suffer." † P. 310.
‡ 1 Cor. 3 : 2 ; Ephes. 2 : 20.

and the best."* We take and apply it just as you have done, to what you state to be the Orthodox claim for the Atonement made by Christ in his sufferings and death, namely, that it was, as the case demanded, an Infinite Atonement; and, this being the test, both with yourself and us, that claim, as you see in common with us, cannot abide it. In this last analysis it is found wanting. God being "impassible," only the Man Christ Jesus made the Atonement; and then, of course, it must be finite, and could be no more. The fact is, that Mr. Griffin evidently felt the force of the sentence quoted above from Channing; and which, though he called and would fain make it appear a mere "Unitarian taunt," he knew under the circumstances had the weight of an argument.†

* P. 43. Before Athanasius, the Patripassian theory, so called from its teaching that the Father himself became man, hungered, thirsted, suffered, and died in Christ, had been broached and advocated by Praxeas and others in the second century.

† How far Mr. Griffin's views have been accepted by the Orthodox, I have not been careful to inquire. Prof. Tayler Lewis, in an elaborate review of Mr. G.'s book, from which I have before quoted, (Bibl. Repos. 3d series, vol. 2, p. 381 et seq.,) while "confessing a strong inclination towards" his theory "in some of its features," says he is "not ashamed to admit an exceeding strong reluctance to adopt any sentiment, on these mysterious subjects, which may even seem to be at variance with the received doctrine of the Church." Afterwards his own language seems sufficiently strong. "It may be maintained, however, that the Church has most distinctly held, without any figure, or any merely constructive use of language, that God did come down to earth, that he did humble himself, that he did become incarnate, that he was born, that he did suffer, that he did die, and that he saved the Church *by his own blood.* All this, to be sure, is generally qualified by a scholastic hypothesis," (the "Athanasian," as Mr. G. calls it, and against which he contends,) "yet still in such a way as to leave the

Finally, we are charged, in our rejection of the orthodox doctrine of the Atonement, with holding out the expectation that men are to be saved by their own holiness, or, as more commonly expressed, by their own merits, rather than by the merits of an Infinite Saviour. To this charge we reply, first, that no Infinite Saviour—unless GOD Himself, the God and Father of our Lord Jesus Christ be meant, as notoriously He is not—is shown. Christ is not, even by virtue of all that he suffered, an Infinite Saviour. As an all-sufficient Saviour, we most gratefully acknowledge and confide in him. Secondly, it is true that we do not rely on the merits or the righteousness of Christ, holy, and blessed, and exalted as he is; or on any mystical

great truth unaffected for all such minds as may be willing humbly to receive the doctrine, and these explicit statements of it, whilst they admit their incapacity to understand the philosophy by which it is sought to be made consistent with other theories. No theologian who has any reputation for soundness would venture to say that this language has been used figuratively, or by way of accommodation. There is, in some way, a most important reality in the affirmation, that God did suffer, which we had better receive without explanation than not to receive at all. He who maintains it in its most literal sense, and rejects all qualification, is certainly nearer the universally received orthodox faith, than one who regards the sufferings of the Redeemer solely in their human relation." Though "the *Church*" has "held" all that Dr. Lewis alleges that it has, it has still "held" it in such a way, that when pressed by Unitarian objections, the language used proved a sham. "GOD did" *not* "suffer"—"HE did" *not* "die." *Christ* suffered—*Christ* died, in his *human* nature, as man. The Scripture—and this we take to be authority paramount to "the Church"—nowhere says that GOD either suffered or died, when our Lord was in agony or expired on the Cross. This is beyond contradiction. "Scholastic" theology has refined, and speculated, and gone wide away from Scripture, till it has got far beyond its depth.

efficacy of his mere blood, or sufferings, or death, or Cross; but, on the other hand, we do not rely upon or trust to any merits or righteousness of our own. "We have not so learned Christ." We are not silly or weak or impious enough, to suppose this the alternative; to think of presenting any claim to the eternal blessedness of Heaven, on the ground of any virtue, goodness, righteousness, holiness of ours, imperfect as it must be at the best, if even the achievement of a full century of years. And yet, that blessedness is the promise of God through Christ; and on

It seems plain enough that Dr. Lewis has a strange *hankering after* Mr. G.'s position, and could he take it, would. But he cannot, and therefore, "in conclusion," he says: "There are exceptions which we might take to a good many passages. We cannot at all agree with the author's extreme view respecting the death of Christ. It seems sufficient, (!) even on his own theory, to regard the Divine Person as actually suffering the agonies which attended the separation of the human soul from the body, without regarding him as laying down his Divine life." Still, he "cannot help regarding it as a most timely and valuable production."

In one place in the extract given above, Dr. Lewis seems to cling to the reading "God" in Acts 20:28. How can he, in face of the overwhelming mass of testimony against it, and in favor of "the Lord"? Does he not know that this latter reading can be traced to the time of Iranæus in the second century; and is found in all the most ancient and valuable MSS. as far back as the Cambridge and the Ephraem both of as high antiquity as the fifth or sixth century, the Alexandrine of the sixth, and Abp. Laud's of the seventh or eighth? I say nothing of the Greek MSS. of less note, or of the oldest versions, or the Fathers, which, in a vast majority, sustain it. Dr. J. P. Smith, in his "Scripture Testimony," speaks of "this remarkable consent of *all* the chief authorities." Olshausen says it is impossible to maintain the "genuineness" of the common reading "consistently with the critical authorities"; and declares that "*all* recent critics recognize 'the Lord' as the right one." I cannot swell this note, already so extended, but refer back to p. 94 in Lect. IV.

that promise we rely as confidently as though God, from the parted heavens, audibly declared it. Our trust is in the free and unpurchased grace, favor, mercy, love of God in Christ; in his holy word declared by our Lord. Better, surer ground of trust we ask not, for none better or surer could we have. But we insist, also, on the authority of both Old and New Testament, that from the first God has made Repentance, Newness of Life, Personal Holiness and Faith, all of them, indispensable conditions of Forgiveness, Acceptance, Salvation. Even after the death of our Lord, after his atonement had been made, remember, the Apostle Paul declared that "God will render to every man according to his deeds"; and James, that "Faith without works is dead."* All this is just as true, just as living and abiding truth, since Christ came, and suffered, and died, and did all that he has done — and he has done all that God required or man needed—as before. Reverently be it said, that those conditions, not even he, the Anointed of God, could have done away. No minister of his Gospel, however orthodox, whatever his theory of the Atonement, whatever efficacy he may ascribe to the Cross of Christ, will dare deny the Scripture declaration—"without holiness no man can see the Lord"! What becomes, then, of this constantly-vaunted sole reliance on an alleged Infinite Atonement!

The Cross of Christ! Blessed seal which the Saviour set to all that his life, teachings, works, solemn

* Ezek. 18 : 30 et seq.; Matt. 7 : 21; Acts 20 : 21; 26 : 20; Rom. 2 : 6; James 2 : 26.

warnings, appeals and promises, exhibited, revealed. enforced! The Cross of Christ! from which men should learn the odiousness of that sin which made necessary so stupendous a sacrifice; which proved his entire self-surrender and obedience to the will of his Father, his perfect trust and faith, patience and resignation. The Cross of Christ! where was illustrated the glory of filial affection and of a holy friendship, of unparalleled magnanimity in forbearance under all injury and insult, and in forgiveness of his enemies in their very act of mocking and murdering him. The Cross of Christ! where an unwavering fortitude, and calm, composed, fervent piety and devoutness of spirit, filled and glorified and closed the scene. God be thanked, when all else has failed, that throughout the ages which have followed our Lord's ascension, the contemplation of that Cross has sent, and will continue to send through all ages to come, a vast and beneficent moral power into the hearts of men! If the blood of bulls and goats under the Mosaic Law cleansed from all outward ritual and legal uncleanness, how much more shall the blood of Christ, that great sacrifice of himself, in which he gave the last and highest proof of obedience to the Father's will, and which was made for our sakes, by its solemn appeal to our sensibility and our gratitude "cleanse our consciences" from all moral and spiritual uncleanness and sin; keep us from all further transgression, and reconcile us to God!*

* See Hebrews 9: 14.

LECTURE X.

CONCLUDING LECTURE—ANTIQUITY AND HISTORY OF UNITARIANISM.

It is very frequently said, probably by those who are unaccustomed to this sort of investigation believed, that Unitarianism is of very recent origin, a very modern doctrine. But I affirm and hope to show that, on the contrary, it is very ancient; nay, the ancient, original, primitive Christianity—the Christianity of Christ. We claim to be Christians; not out of the Church, but in and of the Church, by virtue of holding the original faith of the Saviour and his Apostles. No Protestant, indeed, of any school or denomination, should be satisfied with believing any thing less of the antiquity of his own faith as attested by the Scriptures. A Romanist consistently may. The resort of Tradition and the Custody of the Church are open to him; and though an alleged doctrine be not patent on the face of Scripture, be not by mortals discoverable there, enough for him that in the wisdom of the Saviour it was deemed fit not to publish it so early, but to leave its keeping and transmission to the Church.

Hence we say, that it is not sufficient merely to prove our views to be ancient; it is not the most important thing. They must be shown to be identical with, nay, the very and express teaching of Christ and of his Apostles. They must be throughout Scriptural; squaring with Scripture in all their statements; and this is what I have aimed at showing Unitarianism to be. I know not a point which is peculiar to Unitarianism, or serves to distinguish it from the popular theology, which cannot be expressly stated in the recorded words of the New Testament. Not so with Orthodoxy. Not a Creed in Christendom which expresses its peculiarities is, or possibly can be, stated in the language of Scripture. Attempt to state those peculiarities in that language, and agree to hold by the statement when done, and you will soon find yourself committed to simple, unqualified Unitarianism.

For what, exactly stated, is Christian Unitarianism, but belief in the strict, personal Unity of God; in One God, the Father—the God and Father of our Lord Jesus Christ. Whoever, therefore, accrediting at the same time the special Divine Mission and Authority of Christ, believes that, is a Unitarian Christian. But all Christians agree in holding the Unity of God. True. But, in our view, the Unity is strictly, really, simply Unity; nothing more, nothing less: while in the Trinitarian view it is something more, something else, namely,—a Trinity in Unity, a Unity in Trinity. In this view the Father is God, the Son is God, the Holy Ghost is God; in our view the Father alone is God. Hence the controversy. Again: all Christians agree that Jesus is the Christ, the Son of God. We hold to that, and stop there. But Trinitarians, moreover hold, that he is, nevertheless, very and eternal God; one of three co-equal, co-eternal persons in a Divine Trinity. Hence, in another regard, the controversy. Therefore, the work before us is this; to show, that neither the doctrine of the Trinity as stated in any of the professedly Trinitarian Creeds of Christendom, nor that of the proper Deity or Godhead of Christ, was taught by Christ or by his Apostles, or held by the primitive, catholic or universal Church.

The highest point of Christian antiquity, is, of course, the era of Christ himself, the Divine Founder and Head of the Church; and of the Apostles, the men whom he personally selected, called and empowered to be the heralds of the new faith. To that we go back, and hold and affirm, that neither he, nor they, taught either the doctrine of a Trinity of co-equal persons in the Godhead, nor his own proper Godhead or Supreme Deity.

Having already examined the Scriptural arguments of our Trinitarian brethren, the texts or passages of Scripture which they allege in support of their position, I shall not here repeat myself, but give a single citation from Neander, the great historian of the Church. "The doctrine of the Trinity," he declares,* "is expressly held forth in no one particular passage of the New Testament; for the only one in which this is done, the passage relating to the three that bear record, (1 John 5 : 7,) is undoubtedly spurious, and in its ungenuine shape testifies to the fact, how foreign such a collocation is from the style of the New Testament Scriptures." Higher authority on a point of this sort,

* History of the Chr. Church, (Prof. Torrey's Transl.) vol. i. p. 572.

either on the score of his unquestioned orthodoxy or his vast and thorough learning, those who differ the most from us cannot cite.—From this I turn at once to testimony from the History of the Church.

The "Acts of the Apostles" is the first original document and authority on which that history rests. It was written, be it remembered, by that St. Luke whose "Gospel" stands as the third on the list of our sacred books; a Gospel from which Trinitarians cite not a single text in support of their views. And, in the "Acts," the only history of the earliest period of the Church, bringing it down from the Ascension of our Lord for about thirty years, to St. Paul's imprisonment at Rome, there is not the remotest intimation or hint of either of the doctrines in question, to be pressed into their service. We are thus brought to the year of our Lord, 64, during all which period, certainly, the Church must have been Unitarian.

Thus much is admitted by the early Fathers. They unite in declaring that St. John was the first who even approximated to teaching the proper Deity of Christ.

Origen, A.D. 230, declares that "John alone introduced the knowledge of the eternity of Christ to the minds of the Fathers."* In another place he calls the Gospel of John "the first-fruits" (or most valuable) "of the gospels," because "no one taught the divinity of Christ so clearly as" he.† Eusebius, A.D. 315, says that "John commenced with the doctrine of the Divinity of Christ, as a part reserved for him by the Divine Spirit, as if for a superior."‡ Chrysostom, "the golden-mouthed," lauds John's bold-

* Opp. ii. 428. † Comm. in Johan. ii. 5. ‡ Eccles. Hist. 109.

ness and courage for declaring what his predecessors had only hinted at, and says in reference to the point under discussion: "John alone taught the eternal and super-celestial wisdom." Again: "John first lighted up the lamp of theology"; and again, "Leaving the Father, he discoursed concerning the Son; because the Father was known to all, if not as a Father, yet as God, but the Unbegotten was unknown." Still more: "This doctrine was not published at first, for the world would not receive it. . . . . . John, therefore, the son of thunder, last of all advanced to the doctrine of his (Christ's) divinity, after those three heralds (the first three evangelists); and with great propriety he followed them, and they went before, lightening a little as the lightning precedes the thunder, lest bursting from the clouds at once it should stun the hearer. They therefore lightened the *economy*, or the humanity of Christ, but he thundered out the *theology*";* meaning, the doctrine of the Godhead of Christ.

Ambrose, A.D. 382, says: "If there be any other things which intimate to the intelligent the divinity of Christ, in which he is equal to the Father, John almost alone has introduced them into his Gospel; as having drunk more familiarly, and more copiously, the secret of his divinity from the breast of our Lord, on which he was accustomed to lean at meat."† To the same effect might be cited Jerom, Epiphanius, and others; showing that the writers of those earliest centuries of our era agreed that till John wrote his Gospel, the Divinity, in the sense of the proper Deity of Christ, had not been published to the world, even if known by any of the

* Opp. vi. 235, 604; viii. 2; vi. 171, 173. † Opp. iv. 374.

Apostles. Now, John's, as it is the last in order of the Four Gospels, so it was the last written of them all; and the date of its composition brings us down to A.D. 68, or four years later than the Book of Acts; to which time of course the body of the Church must have been Unitarian. By this I mean, that for the first sixty-eight years of our era, the mass of those who had become converts to our religion under the immediate teaching of our Lord and of his Apostles, knew nothing either of his proper Deity, or of the doctrine of a Trinity of co-equal Persons in the Godhead. And it may be remarked in this connection, and as confirmatory of the ground I occupy, that early in the fourth century, the ecclesiastical historian Eusebius — there being a chasm in the history proper of the Church, or at least no detailed record of it for a period immediately following the close of the "Acts" or A.D. 64 — quotes Hegesippus, a Jewish historian whose works are now lost, as bringing down the history to the middle of the second century. This writer gives, according to Eusebius, a catalogue of the Heresies of his day to the number of twelve, but not one of them involved Unitarian views. He does not even mention the Ebionites, who believed only the doctrine of the simple humanity of Christ. What other inference can be drawn from such a fact, than that it was no heresy, to the middle of the second century at least, to deny or reject the doctrine of the Deity of our Lord?

What, then, was the faith of that early Church, the Church of the first three centuries, and of the Fathers who flourished previous to, or composed the Council of Nice, A.D. 325?

There is no pretence, that before Justin Martyr, A.D. 140, any clear evidence has come down to us of belief in the early Church of even the derived deity of Christ. He was the first, so far as we can discover, distinctly to advance a dogma which proved to be the first fatal step in departure from the simple, primitive faith. That faith held Christ to be divine, only as having pre-existed, or as having been miraculously born, coming on a divine mission, holding a lofty official rank by the special appointment of God. But even Justin held and taught this dogma of Christ's deity, in a manner utterly at variance with the modern idea of the co-equality of the three persons of the Godhead. He speaks of Christ as "next in rank" to God; he says, "Him we reverence next after God"; he declares, that "the Father is the author to him both of his existence and of his being powerful, and of his being Lord and God." Emphatically—"I say, that he never did anything but what *that God who made all things, and above whom there is no God*, willed that he should do and say."* Irenæus, A.D. 178, says: "All the Evangelists have delivered to us the doctrine of One God, and One Christ, the Son of God." And again: "The Father of our Lord Jesus Christ . . . of Him it is that Paul declared: 'There is One God, even the Father, who is above all, and through all, and in us all.'"† Clement of Alexandria, at the close of the second century, calls the Father alone, "without beginning"; and in immediate connection describes

* Apol. i. p. 63, Dial. c. Trypho. pp. 252, 282.

† Lib. ii. cap. 3; iii. cap. 1.

the Son, as "the beginning and first-fruits of things, from whom we must learn the Father of all, the most ancient and beneficent of beings."* In the beginning of the third century, we find Tertullian saying: "If the Father and the Son are to be named together, I call the Father God, and Jesus Christ, Lord; though I can call Christ God, when speaking of himself alone." "The Son is derived from the Father," he adds, "as the branch from the root, the stream from the fountain, the ray from the sun."† Origen, A.D. 230, says: "He who is God of himself, is THE GOD; as the Saviour states in his prayer to the Father, 'that they may know thee, the Only True God'; but whosoever becomes divine, by partaking of His divinity, cannot be styled, THE GOD, but *a God;* among whom, especially, *is the first-born of all creatures.*" And again: "Prayer is not to be directed to one begotten, not even to Christ himself, but to the God and Father of the universe alone, to whom also our Saviour prayed, and to whom he teaches us to pray."‡ Novatus, A.D. 251, says: "The Son, to whom the divinity is communicated, is, indeed, God; but God, the Father of all, is deservedly God of all, and the originating cause of his Son, whom he begat Lord."§ Arnobius, A.D. 300, calls "Christ a God, under the form of a man, speaking by order of the Supreme God;" and says, that "at length, did God Almighty, the Only God, send Christ."‖ Lactantius, A.D. 310, says: "Christ taught that there is One God, alone to be worshipped. Never did he call himself

* Opp p. 700.

† Adv. Prax. c. 8; c. 13.

‡ Comm. ii. p. 47. Opp. tom. i. 222.

§ Cap. 23.

‖ Ad Gen. lib. ii. pp. 50, 57.

God, because he would not have been true to his trust, if, being sent to take away a multiplicity of gods, and to declare One, he had introduced another besides. And because he assumed nothing to himself, that he might obey the commands of him who sent him, he *received* the dignity of Perpetual Priest, the honor of Sovereign King, the power of a Judge, the title of God."*

We have reached the time of the Council of Nice; and the series of testimonies, which I have cited merely as specimens of the manner in which the anti-Nicene and Nicene Fathers expressed themselves, is enough to show that they held views impossible to be reconciled with the received Trinitarian creeds of our day. They uniformly subordinate the Son to the Father, however they may style the former God. They make him a derived and dependent being. They trace all his gifts and powers to the Father. Even the famous Athanasius himself, who at the time of the Council was a young man, and who, about forty years afterwards, led the way for establishing the equality of the Holy Ghost with the Father and the Son—"the true doctrine," as Gregory Nazianzen calls it, in his Eulogy on Athanasius, "of the One Godhead and nature of the Three Persons"—even he, according to Bishop Bull, "concedes that the Father is justly called the only God, because He only is without origin, and is alone the fountain of divinity."† Very learned Trinitarians acknowledge the position for which I am contending, in regard to the theology of the first three centuries. Bishop Bull, whose Defence of the Nicene

* Inst. lib. iv. c. 13.

† Def. Fid. Nic. iv. c. i. § 6.

Creed is regarded as the great reservoir of proofs for the Trinity from Ecclesiastical History, declares, that "No one can doubt, that the Fathers who lived before the Nicene Council, acknowledged this subordination," that is, of the Son, or the Son and Spirit, to the Father; and he proceeds "to show, that the fathers who wrote after this Council, taught the same doctrine."* Mr. Hill criticised this statement, but Bishop Burnet said: "It does not become Mr. Hill to find fault with the Bishop, for having asserted that the Fathers, before the Council of Nice, did conceive in the Trinity a Subordination, importing an Inequality of the two last Persons with the first. The Bishop has but too many proofs upon this Article; and none but those who never read the Ancients, or read them without attention, disown it."† Münscher, in his "Elements of Dogmatic History," says, that "respecting the consummate perfection and majesty of the FATHER, there was no disagreement among" the early Fathers.‡ Cudworth declares, that "the generality of *Christian Doctors*, for the first three hundred years after the Apostles' times, plainly asserted the same subordination."§ M. Jurieu, the French Reformer, alleges, with proof-citations, that the same view was unanimously professed by the fathers of the first three centuries.‖

In the light of these testimonies, what was the faith of the Nicene Council, three hundred and twenty-five years after Christ? It was virtually that, which had

* Def. Fid. Nic. iv. c. i. § 3. † Animadv. on Hill, p. 30.

‡ Murdoch's Translation. § Intell. Sys. vol. ii. p. 417.

‖ Past. Let. p. 126. See also Hagenbach, Hist. of Doctrines, vol. i p. 129.

been held from the time of Justin Martyr by all the ante-Nicene Fathers. It taught, indeed, that the Son was *consubstantial*, or, as the Creed reads in the Book of Common Prayer, "of one substance with the Father." This expression, however, did not mean, of the same numerical, identical substance, but, as Jortin expresses it, "of the same generical substance," a sameness of kind. The Son being of one substance with the Father, was thus declared to be of the same divine nature; and *so far* there was a natural equality between them. "But," says the Trinitarian Jortin, "according to them, (the Nicene fathers,) this natural equality excluded not a relative inequality; a *majority* and *minority*, founded upon the everlasting difference between *giving* and *receiving*, *causing* and *being caused*. . . . When they said, that the Father was *God*, they meant that he was God of *himself, originally* and *underived*. When they said, that the Son was *God*, they meant, that he was God by *generation* or *derivation*."* "What is of the *same nature*," said the great advocate of that early form of Trinitarianism, Athanasius, "is consubstantial"; and he illustrated it by saying, that "one man is of the same nature with another, as regards substance."†

* Jortin's Rem. on Eccles. Hist. ii. p. 202.

† Ep. ii. ad. Serap. Gibbon, who from his infidel position may be considered a disinterested witness on such a point, says, that "those who supported the Nicene doctrine, appeared to consider the expression, *of substance*, as if it had been synonymous with that *of nature*; and they ventured to illustrate their meaning, by affirming that three men, as they belong to the same common species, are consubstantial or homoousian to each other. This pure and distinct equality was tempered on the one hand by the internal connection and spiritual penetration, which indissolubly unite the divine persons, and on the other,

Farther than this, that Council did not go. Before it sat, the highest views held by any of Christ, held him to be inferior, subordinate to God, the Father. Hence no co-equal Trinity, no Tri-Personality in the One God, no Trinity in Unity and Unity in Trinity; no Supreme Deity of Christ, as we nowadays hear. And in this very Council, the Supremacy of the Father, and thus the essence of the Unitarian faith, was after all sustained, as we shall the better see when we come to examine the terms of the Creed itself.

But this term, "consubstantial," by and by came to signify, not simply *sameness* of nature, but individual *identity*. Accordingly, after the middle of the fourth century, instead of the Supremacy of the Father, and the real, unqualified Subordination and Inferiority of the Son,—by virtue of which statement they were of necessity two distinct beings,—their actual numerical identity was taught. How true it is, as I have before had occasion to remark, and as will appear still clearer as I proceed, that systematic theology is but the piling up of doctrines, nay, of mere human opinions, one upon another, until the simple teachings of the Scripture,

by the pre-eminence of the Father, which was acknowledged as far as it is compatible with the independence of the Son. Within these limits the almost invisible and tremulous ball of Orthodoxy was allowed securely to vibrate. On either side, beyond this consecrated ground, the heretics and the dæmons lurked in ambush, to surprise and devour the unhappy wanderer. But as the degrees of theological hatred depend on the spirit of the war, rather than on the importance of the controversy, the heretics who degraded, were treated with more severity, than those who annihilated the person of the Son."—Milman's Gibbon's Hist. Decl. and Fall of Roman Empire. Boston ed. 1850, vol. ii. 320.

the Christianity of Christ, is well nigh covered from sight by the accretions of human speculation!

Let us now examine the early Creeds. And first, though the Scriptures set forth no formal creed of the nature of those symbols of Faith which subsequently obtained in various branches of the Church, and which have continued to be manufactured in modern times, they do in various passages enunciate very distinctly and emphatically what in this connection must be deemed and taken to be, fundamental articles of our holy religion. Ascending, then, to the highest, because, as we believe, divinely prompted, and authoritative statements on matters of faith, those of the Master and Lord of Christians, what do we find? A scribe asked him: "'Which is the first commandment of all?' And Jesus answered him: 'The first of all the commandments is, The Lord our GOD is ONE Lord. . . . . This is the first commandment. . . . . There is none other commandment greater.'" When the Scribe rejoined, and "said unto him, 'Well, Master, thou hast said the truth; for *there is One God;* and there is *none other* but He'"—the record proceeds to tell us that "Jesus saw that he answered discreetly, and said unto him, 'Thou art not far from the kingdom of God.'"* In that remarkable prayer which our Lord addressed to the Father just before he went forth to his betrayal, how explicit his language—"THIS IS LIFE ETERNAL, THAT THEY MIGHT KNOW THEE, THE ONLY TRUE GOD, AND JESUS THE CHRIST, WHOM THOU HAST SENT!"† So explicit—so luminous—so free

* Mark 12: 29–32.

† John 17: 3.

from, nay, so absolutely precluding a thought of any, the least ambiguity in itself, or doubt as to its significance on the part of the reader, that to attempt to expound it, would seem as absurd as "to gild refined gold."

From the Master, turn to the disciple. When Jesus asked, "'Whom say ye that I am?' Simon Peter answered and said, 'Thou art the CHRIST, the SON of the living GOD.'" How emphatic the approval which our Lord pronounced: "Blessed art thou, Simon, son of Jonas! For flesh and blood hath not revealed it unto thee, but my Father which is in heaven."* The same disciple, on another occasion, addressed to his Master these words: "Thou hast the words of Eternal Life: and we believe and are sure, that Thou art that Christ, the Son of the Living God."† Again; his Master had risen from the dead and ascended to heaven; and—said Peter to the wondering witnesses, in his speech at Pentecost: "Therefore, being by the right hand of God exalted, and having received of the Father the promise of the Holy Ghost, he hath shed forth this, which ye now see and hear." He then adds to this language—of itself plain and significant enough to the most ordinary mind, one would think, as indicating Christ's dependence and the Spirit's also—this closing proclamation: "Therefore, let all the house of Israel know assuredly, that GOD hath *made* that same *Jesus* whom ye have crucified, *both Lord and Christ!*"‡ And yet once more—at Cesarea, the same Apostle declared, before a Gentile audience, that "God anointed

* Matt. 16: 15–17. † John 6: 68, 69. ‡ Acts 2: 33–36.

Jesus of Nazareth with the Holy Ghost and with power. . . . . for God was with him."*

Not a whit less distinct was the creed of Paul. To the Corinthian Church he writes: "Though there be that are called gods, whether in heaven or in earth, (as there be gods many and lords many,) to us there is but ONE GOD, the FATHER, of whom are all things and we in Him; and One Lord, Jesus Christ, by whom are all things and we by him."† Again, to the Ephesians: "One Lord, one faith, one baptism; ONE GOD and FATHER of all, who is *above all*, and through all, and in you all."‡ I cannot forbear citing again, in this connection, that memorable passage in his first Epistle to the Corinthians, in which it would almost seem that Paul meant to guard his readers against imagining that Christ's kingly office was of independent and eternal or perpetual authority. "Then cometh the end when he (Christ) shall have delivered up the kingdom to GOD, even the FATHER; when he shall have put down all rule and all authority and power. For he (Christ) must reign, till He (God) hath put all enemies under his feet. The last enemy that shall be destroyed is death. For 'He (God) hath put all things under his feet.' But when it is said 'all things are put under him,' it is manifest that He is excepted which did put all things under him. And when all things shall be subdued unto him, then shall the Son also himself be subject unto Him that put all things under him, that GOD may be all in all."§

* Acts 10: 38. † 1 Ep. 8: 5, 6. ‡ 4: 5, 6
§ 1 Epistle 15: 24–28.

Finally, when the Chamberlain of the Ethiopian Queen was converted by Philip, he asked: "What doth hinder me to be baptized?" And the reply of Philip was: "If thou believest with all thine heart, thou mayest." And the Creed, the confession of faith which he made and Philip accepted, was: "I believe that Jesus Christ is the Son of God!" That was all. No Trinity, no Godhead of Christ, or of the Holy Ghost. Nor is either of these things to be found, or in the remotest way hinted at or shadowed forth, in any of the words of our Lord or his disciples which I have cited. Nay, no words, his or theirs, can be cited from Holy Writ, contradictory to, or at variance with them. His divine Sonship, Messiahship, Kingship, Lordship, are expressly claimed, recognized, declared; but never his Godhead or Deity, in these Scriptural Creeds or Statements of Faith.

True, as the word is commonly used—a use, by the way, which has excited a very unhappy prejudice, I often think, against the thing—there are in the New Testament no *Creeds*. Our Lord and his Apostles prescribed no set Articles of Faith, no carefully-drawn Symbol, to be through all time subscribed and transmitted as of binding authority upon his Universal Church. We find here and there a "*Credo*," an "*I believe*," in which an individual expresses his faith in "the Christ, the Son of God," and a "Blessed art thou" follows it. But nothing beyond, except that it is placed on the holy record and sent down the stream of time, for the example, instruction, guidance of after ages. When, however, we leave the Scriptures, and open the History of the Church after the age of inspiration and miracle had passed, we at once meet with Creeds, Symbols, Declarations of Faith; mostly drawn up and voted in by General Councils, as they were called, summoned together by the edict of an Emperor; who, though styled Christian, knew as much, and often cared as much about the merits of the discussion, as the most stupid slaves at his feet. These Councils were to settle the points in dispute, and establish the faith of the Church.*

* How far deference should be paid to the decisions of such Councils my readers may be aided in judging by the following extract from Dr. Jortin, one of the lights of the English Establishment, of course a Trinitarian, but a most candid and able writer.

"Consider a little by what various motives these various men may be influenced; as, by reverence to the Emperor, or to his Councillors and favorites, his slaves and eunuchs; by fear of offending some great Prelate, as a Bishop of Rome or of Alexandria, who had it in his power to insult, vex, and plague all the bishops within and without his jurisdiction; by the dread of passing for heretics, and of being calumniated, reviled, hated, anathematised, excommunicated, imprisoned, banished, fined, beggared, starved, if they refused to submit; by compliance with some active, leading, and imperious spirits, by a deference to a majority, by a love of dictating and domineering, of applause and respect, by vanity and ambition, by a total ignorance of the question in debate, or a total indifference about it, by private friendships, by enmity and resentment, by old prejudices, by hopes of gain, by an indolent disposition, by good nature, by the fatigue of attending, and a desire to be at home, by the love of peace and quiet, and a hatred of contention, etc.

"Whosoever takes these things into due consideration, will not be disposed to pay a blind deference to the authority of General Councils, and will rather be inclined to judge that 'the Council held by the Apostles was the first and the last in which the Holy Spirit may be affirmed to have presided.' . . . . If such Councils make right-

Before, however, the age of these Councils, we find in Irenæus of Lyons, who flourished near the close of the second century, and in Tertullian of Carthage a few years later, statements of the ancient faith largely resembling those of what is commonly called the Apostles' Creed. That Creed in form, is not found earlier than in Rufinus of Aquileia at the close of the fourth century, who transmitted a tradition which had reached him, that it was actually composed by the Apostles before they separated to their missionary work. The tradition kept its hold on the Latin Church till the Reformation, when its Apostolic origin began to be questioned by Erasmus and others, and now in the words of Sir Peter King, "All learned persons are agreed, that it was never composed by the Apostles."* It is as Bunsen expresses it, "an epitome of the leading facts related in the Gospel as to the Father, Son, and Spirit." He adds: "It has no value but its faithfulness, and no authority but that of its origin. Still the point round which these epitomised elements have crystallised is that, which constitutes the whole doctrinal consciousness of the ancient Church: the belief in the Father, the Son, and the Spirit.

This, in the mind of the Primitive Church, was the only real doctrinal point respecting which the historical records of Christianity are in the highest sense authoritative. Again he says: "The most remarkable and important character of the Apostles' Creed is

eous decrees, it must have been by strange good luck."—Notes on Eccles. History, vol. ii. 183–4.

* Const. of the Prim. Church, Pt. ii. p. 57.

consequently this, that it purports to be nothing but an epitome of the New Testament based upon the belief in that divine threefoldness."* Mark that word of this most learned scholar, and competent critic, the Chevalier Bunsen — "*threefoldness*" — nay, "divine threefoldness"; and he a Trinitarian. If this "divine threefoldness" be all that is required to be believed in order to be orthodox, Unitarians should be esteemed such. Nay, here is just the point. We never have disputed this "divine threefoldness." What we have disputed and denied, and what we do still dispute and deny, is the Trinity as held in modern times and in our own day, in the forms of Tri-unity, Tri-personality, a Trinity in Unity and Unity in Trinity, in the Godhead. We deny that according to the teachings of Christ and his Apostles, God exists in Three co-equal, co-eternal Persons. We affirm that He exists in One Person, revealed by our Lord as the Father. All the while we assent to and believe, with the Supreme Deity of the Father, the divinity of the Son and of the Holy Spirit. We take up, then, the so-called "Apostles' Creed," admitting it to be the most ancient formal creed extant—and what does it say?

"I believe in God, the Father Almighty; and in Jesus Christ His only-begotten Son, our Lord; who was born of the Virgin Mary by the Holy Ghost; was crucified under Pontius Pilate; buried; arose from the dead on the third day; ascended to the heavens, and sits at the right hand of the Father, whence he

* Hippolytus, vol. ii. p. 93.

will come to judge the living and the dead; and in the Holy Spirit, the holy Church, the remission of sins, and the resurrection of the body."

This is the form given by Dr. Murdoch in a note to his edition of Mosheim's Ecclesiastical History,* as "the common form of it in the fourth century"; and where will you find in it a word, a hint, of any thing contrary to Christian Unitarianism? You cannot. It is simply and entirely Unitarian. The "divine threefoldness" is there; but "the Father Almighty" is alone styled "God." Not a word, not a hint of the Personality of the Holy Spirit, or of the Deity of Christ, who is described as "the only-begotten Son" of God, and "our Lord." Coleridge thought it "might be possible to deduce the Catholic doctrine of the Trinity" from it; but admitted, that "assuredly it is not fully expressed therein." . . "It has," he says in another place, "it appears to me, indirectly (why not directly?) favored Arianism and Socinianism."† Well is it remarked by Mr. Wilson—"A Trinity, such as is

* Vol. i. p. 80. It is remarkable that in the notices of it in Irenæus, and Tertullian a little later, the first clause invariably reads "*One* God."—Sir Peter King says, that "in all the most primitive Creeds (he means forms of this creed) whether Latin or Greek, this article runs "I believe in *One* God" or "in the *Only* God." (Hist. Apostles' Creed, p. 50.) So Bishop Pearson, Exposition of the Creed, Art. i. p. 32. Bunsen gives us the following, as the "Primitive Form" of the Ante-Nicene Creed of the Church of Alexandria, of which Church Athanasius was at a later period bishop:

"I believe in the only true God, the Father Almighty:
And in his only-begotten Son Jesus Christ, our Lord and Saviour:
And in the Holy Spirit, the Giver of Life."—Hippolytus, vol. ii.p. 97.

† Works, vol ii. pp. 229.

acknowledged by Christian Unitarians, may be easily deduced from this Creed; but how it can be possible to deduce from it Trinitarianism, or a Trinity of Persons in the Godhead, is to us as inconceivable as it would be to infer this dogma from the simple declaration of the Apostle Peter, that God anointed Jesus of Nazareth with the holy Spirit and with power."* Dr. Bushnell explicitly says: "If we examine the history of these first ages, we find them speaking, in the utmost simplicity, of the Father, Son, and Holy Ghost; but having still, confessedly, no speculative theory or dogmatic scheme of Trinity. The word, in fact, is not yet invented. . . . If you desire to see the form in which they summed up the Christian truth, you have it in what is called the Apostles' Creed. This beautiful compend was gradually prepared or accumulated in the age prior to theology; most of it, probably, in the time of the Apostolic Fathers.‡ It is purely historic—a simple compendium of Christian fact, without a trace of what we call doctrine; that is, nothing is drawn out into speculative propositions, or pro-

* John Wilson's "Unitarian Principles," etc. (a most valuable work) p. 261. Prof. Schaff, also, in his "History of the Primitive Church," declares the Apostles' Creed to be "trinitarian in structure"; and says that it "gradually grew" out of "the *trinitarian* baptismal formula"! p. 121. Trinitarians must be hard pushed, when the mere juxtaposition of terms, viz. of Father, Son, and Holy Ghost in a paragraph, is used for such a tremendous conclusion as that doctrine of the Trinity which this learned scholar holds.

‡ So called, from having lived and conversed with Apostles. They are six in number; Barnabas the companion of St. Paul; Clement, Bishop of Rome; Hermas; Ignatius Bishop of Antioch; Polycarp "the blessed," as Irenæus styles him, Bishop of Smyrna; and Papias,

pounded as a dogma, in terms of science."* I repeat that this Creed is strictly Unitarian; and shows, in addition to the other testimonies before brought from the Fathers, how truly Unitarian the early centuries were. If there was any Trinity in the Church, then, it must have been what Wilson not inaptly terms—"The Unitarian Trinity"; the doctrine of the Father, the Son, and the Holy Ghost, taught and held from the beginning, and held firmly by us to this day in "its native and beautiful simplicity," and apart from "all vain subtilties, all mysterious researches, every thing that was beyond the reach of common capacities." These are the words of Mosheim, attesting the fact that the Apostles' Creed comprehended "the Christian system" as inculcated by its early teachers. Afterwards, when the historian comes to the beginning of the fourth century and the great controversy which then arose, his language is very distinct and remarkable. "The subject of this fatal controversy, which kindled such deplorable divisions in the Christian world, was the

the companion of Polycarp. The first in order of the Christian writers, any of whose works have come down to us, is Justin Martyr, A.D. 140, about twenty years after the last above named.

* God in Christ, pp. 286, 287. Dr. B. speaks of the word "trinity" as not "yet invented." Theophilus of Antioch, near the close of the second century, was, as I have before mentioned, the first to use the Greek word *τριάς*; "but," Hagenbach says, "not in the ecclesiastical sense of the term "Trinity." This triad of Theophilus was simply the Father, Son, and Spirit, as they appear in the "baptismal formula," and in Paul's benediction, 2 Cor. 13 : 14. Near the same time Tertullian at Carthage introduced the Latin word *trinitas*; which Hagenbach says, "has a more comprehensive doctrinal import." Hist. of Doctrines, vol. i. p. 128.

doctrine of *three persons* in the Godhead; a doctrine which, in the three preceding centuries, had happily escaped the vain curiosity of human researches, and been left undefined and undetermined by any particular set of ideas."*

I pass now to the Nicene Creed. This was adopted by the famous Council assembled by command of the Emperor Constantine at Nice, in the year 325. In the Book of Common Prayer of the Episcopal Church, the second of the Creeds is often called the Nicene Creed; but in exact truth it is a combination of the Nicene and Constantinopolitan Creeds, with some later additions; the latter Creed having been adopted in the year 381. All beyond the words "Holy Ghost" is from the latter.

In the first place, then, this Creed declares explicitly the doctrine of one Almighty God thus:

"We believe in One God, the Father Almighty, Maker of all things visible and invisible."†

It then says of the Son:

"And in One Lord Jesus Christ, the Son of God, begotten, the only-begotten of the Father; that is, of the substance of the Father, God of God, Light of Light, true God of true God, begotten, not made, consubstantial with the Father; by whom all things were made, both in heaven and in earth; who for us men,

* Eccles. Hist. vol. i. pp. 149, 314.

† See the original Creed in Gieseler's Text-Book of Eccl. His. vol. i. p. 297. n. 7. Harper's ed. 1857. "The 'One God,'" says Gieseler, "is here the Father alone, consequently the sameness of essence between Him and the Son is not a numerical unity of essence."

and for our salvation, descended and was incarnate, and was made man, suffered, and rose again on the third day, ascended into the heavens, and will come to judge of the living and the dead."

Remark, that Christ is here expressly, and in exact accordance with Scripture, called "Lord." Next, he is said to be "begotten"; a significant intimation of his subordination to Him who begat. Next, he is described as at most, "God *of* God . . . . true God *of* true God"; and every tyro in Greek knows that the preposition εκ here rendered *of*, expresses the derived origin of the person spoken of, and is often so used in the New Testament;* therefore, God *out of* or *from* God—thus distinctly marking his derived and of course subordinate being. Next, "of the substance of . . . . *consubstantial* with the Father." Now here was the very point of dispute between Arius and Athanasius at the Council of Nice, and to settle which this Council was called; but even Athanasius, as we have already seen, and whose party triumphed, meant only by consubstantial—*of the same nature*, but by no means individual oneness or identity.† This sameness of nature constituted the only equality of the Father and the Son which the Nicenians asserted. In all this, the inferiority and subordination of the Son is apparent; and although it be acknowledged that they decided Christ to be God, they made him nevertheless a derived, and not a self-existent God.

* See Robinson's Lex. of N. T. p. 243. Schleusner's Lex. in N. T. h. v.

† Vid. supra. p. 233.

Of the Holy Ghost, the Creed, in its original form, merely says: "And (we believe) in the Holy Ghost." Nothing is said of its deity or Godhead. That point had not yet been reached.*

What, then, is proved down to the year of our Lord 325? First, that the Church, down to the writing of our fourth Gospel, or A.D. 68—the Church, as it existed from the beginning, and as it grew up in the immediate charge of the Apostles of its Divine Founder and Head—knew nothing of the doctrine of the Trinity of Persons in the Godhead, or of his proper, underived Deity. This, strictly speaking, is the only primitive, Apostolic Church; and this was simply and purely Unitarian. Next, that the Fathers, Ante-Nicene and Nicene, asserted a real subordination, and of course, a real inferiority of the Son to the Father. Next, that they did not hold the proper eternity of the Son as of a real person, or individual, conscious being; but rather, as of an attribute or property of the Father. And lastly, they denied that the Son was numerically or identically the same being with the Father; none of them holding any thing beyond this, that he had

* The original Creed closes with this anathema: "Those who say that there was a time when the Son of God was not, and that before he was begotten he was not, and that he was made out of nothing, or out of another substance or being, and is created, is changeable or alterable, the Catholic Church anathematises." But Gieseler remarks (see the reference in the previous note)—"Even here the sentiment that the Son exists *by the will of the Father*, and *is less than He*, is not spoken against." The anathema was directed in the most exact terms against Arius and his party, who denied the *consubstantialness* or sameness of nature of the Son with the Father; and who insisted that he was made out of nothing, and, of course, though the first and highest, a created being.

the same generic nature with the Father, that is, as a human child is of the same nature with his parent. System or Creed-making had ventured one step towards thorough-going Trinitarianism — the Deification of Christ in this derivative and subordinate sense.

Councils, or Synods, as the Greek word is, were now the rage. In the fourth century no less than forty-five were held, and the strife of party became as embittered as that of the worst modern political cabal.* Constantine seconded the anathema of the Nicene Council; banished Arius into a remote Illyrian province; ordered his writings to be burned, and all who possessed and attempted to conceal, or did not at once produce and cast them into the flames, to death.† But in three years afterwards he recalled Arius and his friends, and would probably have loaded him with honors had not the Presbyter suddenly died soon after his return. His son, Constantius, who finally alone held his throne, favored the Arian party. The tables were now turned, but persecution had, alas! only changed hands. "The Christian religion," says a cotemporary Roman Historian, and an eye-witness and observer of what was doing, "which, in itself, is plain and simple, Constantius confounded by the dotage of superstition. In-

* "Thirteen Councils against Arius, fifteen for him, and seventeen for the Semi-Arians." (Jortin, ii. 210.) The Semi-Arians wished "that the doctrine of Christ's divinity should be settled only in such general expressions as had hitherto satisfied the Christian want, so that, with regard to the difference which divided the two contending parties, nothing was to be defined, and each might be allowed to interpret the language according to its own meaning."—Neander, Hist. of the Church, vol. ii. p. 373.

† Jortin, ii. 205.

stead of reconciling the parties by the weight of his authority, he cherished and propagated, by verbal disputes, the differences which his vain curiosity had excited. The highways were covered with troops of bishops galloping from every side to the assemblies, which they call Synods; and while they labored to reduce the whole sect (of Christians) to their own particular opinions, the public establishment of the posts was almost ruined by their hasty and repeated journeys."* For nearly a half century Unitarianism, in the form of Arianism, was the established religion of the Empire.

It was in such a state of things, as the fruit of a controversy which rent Christendom in pieces, and much in accordance with the prevailing philosophy of the age, that having established the deity of the Son even in the qualified sense we have seen, the next step should be taken towards completing the dogma of the Trinity, namely, the deification of the Holy Ghost. This was done, as has been shown, at the Council of Constantinople, A.D. 381; concerning which says Mosheim: "A hundred and fifty bishops, who were present at this Council, gave the finishing touch to what the Council of Nice had left imperfect; and fixed, in a full and determinate manner, the doctrine of three persons in one God, which is as yet received among the generality of Christians."† But Mosheim, as I have had occasion to remark before, is too hasty. "The finishing touch" was much later. This Trinity

* Gibbon, vol. ii. p. 330; who thus translates from Ammianus, xxi 16.

† History of the Church, vol. i. p. 326.

was a work of time. A doctrine so mysterious, so self-contradictory, not patent on the face of Scripture, was only by degrees forced on the faith of the Church. The Nicene Creed stopped with saying: "We believe in the Holy Ghost." The Creed of Constantinople declared: "We believe in the Holy Ghost, the Lord and Giver of life; who proceedeth from the Father; who, with the Father and Son together is worshipped and glorified; who spake by the prophets."* Here distinctly appears the Personality of the Spirit; and its Deity as a joint object of worship. But the Creed says that it "proceedeth from the Father" only; and in less than fifty years "the unity and equality of the persons which necessarily resulted from holding sameness of essence," and which "was not fully acknowledged at once even by the Nicenians, but continued to be more clearly perceived, was at last expressed by Augustine for the first time with decided logical consequence."† Augustine died A.D. 430; and in a little more than a century of constant strife thereafter, A.D. 589, the third Council of Toledo added the clause, "and the Son" to the Creed, and anathematised all who disbelieved the doctrine it conveyed. Thenceforth it read—"who proceedeth from the Father and the Son"; an alteration which, says Hagenbach, "afterwards led to the disruption between the eastern and western Churches."

Still the modern doctrine of the Trinity was not complete. But without attempting to follow the growth

* Gieseler gives the Creed in its original Greek form, vol. i. 312, n. 35.

† Gieseler, vol. i. 313. See also Neander, ii. pp. 421–423. Hagenbach, Hist. of Doct. i. 282.

of it through the various and tedious disputes which from time to time continued to arise, it is enough to say that "the finishing touch" was reserved for the fourth Council of Lateran, so late as A.D. 1215; that Council to which belongs the baleful preëminence of having established the monstrous dogma of Transubstantiation, ordered the extermination of heretics, and by its persecuting edicts, laid the foundation of the Inquisition. By such a Council was the modern doctrine of the Trinity completed, and for the first time by authority proclaimed as the faith of the Church; that doctrine, in the words of Cudworth, of a "Trinity of Persons numerically the same, or having all one and the same singular existent essence; a doctrine which seemeth not to have been owned by any public authority in the Christian Church, save that of the Lateran Council only."*

Meanwhile, Unitarianism, in its Arian form at least, notwithstanding the exterminating edicts of the Emperor Theodosius, near the close of the fourth century, and cotemporaneous with the Council of Constantinople, continued to struggle on in the hearts of faithful men. At length, about the middle of the seventh century, under the full and cruel effects of those edicts, it for a time sunk from observation. Thenceforward to the Reformation in the sixteenth century were the "Dark Ages"; during which the power of the so-called Catholic Church became despotic, and by and by rioted unchecked in its haughty and ruthless career.

But the Reformation came, and in its early years, Unitarianism revived again in Germany, Switzerland, Transylvania, and Poland. The old spirit of persecu-

* Intellec. System. ii. 435, 436. Lond. ed. 1845.

tion revived with it, and some of the Reformers were its most cruel agents. Michael Servetus, condemned to death at Vienna by Romish Inquisitors, for avowing and publishing it to the world, fled to Geneva, the city of Calvin, only there to be re-arrested, and at his instance, as a heretic; and after a protracted trial, he was, through Calvin's influence, sentenced to the stake, and was actually burned just without the city walls at Champet, by a slow fire of green wood. The celebrated Italians, Lelius Socinus, and Faustus his nephew, were among its most conspicuous advocates. The latter, after his uncle's death at Zurich, in 1578, was invited to Transylvania, where he found a band of disciples true to its simple faith. In 1579 he established himself in Poland, whose famous University at Racow, then in the hands of Unitarians, once boasted of more than a thousand students from various parts of the civilized world, with some of the most distinguished European scholars in its faculty. There he commanded for a time an immense influence; but in 1598 was mobbed, his papers burned, and himself dragged through the streets. Six years afterwards he died peaceably in a retired village in the vicinity of the ancient capital of the kingdom. His works, replete with critical learning, fill two folio volumes; and form a part of the "*Fratres Poloni*," or "Polish Brothers," a collection of theological writings by learned Polish Unitarians of that day, conspicuous among a large and intrepid body of believers in and defenders of Unitarianism in that country. These, in mass, were subsequently expelled from Poland, and found refuge and a home in Transylvania. There their descendants are found, and faithful to their ancient faith to this day. While in Genĕva, the chair of Calvin in the University founded by himself, and the pulpit in which he preached, are filled by a Unitarian Professor and a Unitarian preacher; and Unitarianism is the religion of the state. Of Great Britain and our own country I need not speak at length. Enough to say, that added to our own Congregational or Independent body of churches in either country, are to be added the "Christians," Universalists, a large division of the Friends, the Swedenborgians, the Campbellites, and a part of the Seventh-day Baptists; all Anti-Trinitarians; all advocates of the strict personal Unity of God.

I trust, I have said enough to show that Christian Unitarianism is not a novel, as many seem to suppose, but an ancient form of Christian faith. Nay, we go farther. We claim, that it is the most ancient, the Primitive, the Apostolic Christian Faith; the faith, pre-eminently, which Christ and his Apostles preached; coeval with, nay, the original Christianity. Our text-book is that same Holy Bible to which all consistent Protestants ultimately appeal; while we especially cling to the New Testament, as distinctively, pre-eminently, authoritatively, the rule of faith and practice to the Universal Church of Christ. To that inspired record, first and chiefly; and then, to Christian History and Antiquity, to the history of the Church in the Three First Centuries of our era, written though it be by Trinitarian scholars of highest note, do we appeal, for the sanction and confirmation of our theological position and claims. And though far from thinking, that great names are any positive proof of the truth of any form of religious belief, that surely cannot be a despicable faith which holds on the roll of its confessors and advocates, names like those of the discoverer of gravitation, of the great master of modern intellectual philosophy, of the sublimest of modern bards, and preachers and philanthropists than whom the world has known none greater or purer. Such names as Newton, and Locke, and Milton, and Channing, are a glory to any church.

But it is said, that we do not agree on all points. What sect, what denomination, what church, does? Perfect agreement, entire uniformity, is a thing not to be looked for. Unity of faith, on every point controverted among believers, or which by possibility may be started by inquiring minds, is the merest dream; unity of spirit, the only substantial and commanding reality. "The unity of the spirit, in the bond of peace," is that for which all who acknowledge Jesus to be the Christ, the Son of God, should pray and strive. Fundamentals—doctrines which are the foundation, and therefore the essentials of Christian faith—are not, surely, points of difference, but of agreement, among those who alike confess him to be Lord. They are, they must be those, which are common to all Christian believers, universally accepted by all in every age of the Church. Especially must this be admitted by all who stand on the sufficiency of the Scriptures, and the right of private judgment, the cardinal principles of the Reformation. We value as highly as any believers, the Christian name. We cling to it as tenaciously. We claim it boldly. We are, and of right are, I repeat, say what others may, IN and OF the Church of Christ. That must be a power not known in this age, or this land, certainly, which can expel us. We believe, we rejoice in Christianity as a *spirit;* but we know as well, and believe as strongly, what no sophism or mysticism can make null or do away, that it is a *truth*, God's Truth, also. We desire and pray, that we may cherish the Spirit; but we will hold and "earnestly contend for" the Truth, too.

In the serious and careful review which I have endeavored to take of the topics before me, I have been gratified to find how numerous and how great, during my more than thirty years in the ministry, have been the modifications and concessions of orthodoxy; and almost equally surprised to find my own mind confirmed at every step, and resting not only with unshaken but with increased, nay, with the entirest confidence, in substantially the very doctrinal views of the Gospel which I long ago received and preached. So far as doctrines are concerned, they are, I more and more verily believe, the essence of that Christianity which at the first and from the first constituted the Gospel, the divinely attested and authoritative Gospel of our Lord and Saviour, Jesus Christ; simple, intelligible, harmonious, eminently practical and Scriptural. Briefly, then, let me declare them; and beg those who have followed me so long and so patiently in this discussion, to compare them with Holy Scripture.

Christian Unitarianism affirms in the first place—That there is One only God; that He is one Person, One Being; that He is the God and Father of our Lord Jesus Christ, the God and Father of all mankind. It lays stress not only on the strict personal Unity of God, but especially on His Divine Fatherhood. "To us, there is but One God, the Father."*

* 1 Cor. 8 : 6.

In the second place it affirms—That Jesus is the promised CHRIST; the Divinely-appointed Messiah or Anointed of God; pre-eminently the Son of God, pre-eminently the Son of Man: the most distinguished Messenger and Representative, the brightest visible Manifestation of the Invisible God; second only to God in the glory of that office and rank with which He has invested him; one with God by a moral union and harmony of wisdom, will, holiness, and love; acting with the delegated power and authority of the Supreme; by His indwelling Spirit given him without measure, the infallible Teacher of God's holy Truth; and exalted with the right hand of God to be a Prince and All-sufficient Saviour, to give repentance and forgiveness of sins. "To us there is . . . ONE LORD, JESUS THE CHRIST."*

In the third place it affirms—That the Holy Ghost or Holy Spirit, is the SPIRIT of GOD; not a distinct person, or person at all; but by and through which, God is always present with us and ready to help, inspire, succor, comfort, enlighten, and sanctify the spirits of His children, will they but seek the precious Gift.†

In the fourth place it affirms—That all men are born innocent; free at birth from all taint of sin and guilt, as they are destitute of holiness; gifted with a nature of glorious capacities, but exposed to temptation, liable to sin, actually sinners; needing the provision which God in His abounding mercy has seen fit to make in the Gospel of His Son for their regeneration and salvation; but free to choose, and therefore, free to accept or reject the offered grace.

* 1 Cor. 8 : 6. † Luke 11 : 13.

In the fifth place it affirms—That the Atonement—At-one-ment—is the Reconciliation of man to God; not of God to man, for that could not be necessary. As the All-gracious FATHER, He never needed to be reconciled to his human family; but on the contrary, as the crowning expression of his exhaustless compassion and boundless Love, He sent His only-begotten Son into the world, to teach and bear witness to the truth, to labor, suffer, and die for us, that we might live through him.* The divine instructions, the miraculous works, the sinless and perfect life and example, the sufferings and death, the Resurrection, Ascension, and present Intercession of Christ, being all part and parcel of the means appointed in the counsels of the Infinite Mind, for accomplishing this great Reconciliation and Salvation of the world.†

In the sixth place, it affirms—That the BIBLE is the History and Record of God's Revelations to our race; furnishing, especially in the New Testament, the Divine, and therefore sufficient Rule of Faith and Practice to all Christian Believers; the Holy and inestimable Volume, which the Inspiration and Providence of God have caused to be written, preserved, and transmitted, for the Religious Instruction of mankind in every succeeding age.

Finally, it affirms—That the present is a life of moral discipline and probation, introductory and preparatory to a higher and an eternal life, in which a righteous judgment and retribution await all, and God will render to every man according to his deeds.

* 1 John 4 : 9.

† Rom. 5 : 10; 8 : 30; 2 Cor. 5: 18, 19.

Thus much for the positive or affirmative side. But while thus on the one hand, in contradistinction to all systems of mere Naturalism or Rationalism, Christian Unitarianism affirms the reality of God's last and fullest revelation in and by Christ and his Gospel, and these as the chief and leading doctrines of that Gospel; on the other, in contradistinction to the popular or received Orthodoxy of the Church, it denies and rejects the following dogmas, viz.:

1st. A Tri-personal God, or Three co-equal, co-eternal Persons in the Godhead.

2d. The Supreme Deity of our Lord and Saviour Jesus Christ. It holds, asserts, maintains as earnestly as any form of faith in the Christian Church, his Divinity—his Divine Mission, Office, and Authority; but denies that he is God over all, the Supreme and Eternal God.

3d. The Personality and Deity of the Holy Ghost or Holy Spirit; denying that it is literally a Person; or God in any sense, except as the spirit of a man is the man himself.

4th. The expiatory, vicarious, and infinite Atonement of Christ; with the entire doctrinal scheme of Calvin.

Unitarianism denies and rejects all these dogmas, as gross corruptions of the pure, simple, original Gospel of the Lord—the Christianity of Christ, and of the primitive, Apostolic Church.

Thus much for the negative side. Upon other points, Unitarians, recognizing in others and claiming for themselves the right of private judgment, do not entirely agree, viz.:—

I. As to the metaphysical nature of Christ.

1st. Some believe him to have pre-existed, the first in order of time of all created intelligences;—

2d. Some believe him to have been born of Mary, but miraculously conceived;—

3d. And some rest on his own declaration for the present, and await God's pleasure for further light;—"No man (no one) knoweth who the Son is, but the Father."*

II. As to the Future Punishment of Sin. While they agree in rejecting the popular belief in the eternal damnation of the impenitent, and all believe in a righteous judgment and retribution hereafter;—

1st. Some believe, that the sufferings or punishment of the impenitent will terminate in their annihilation;—

2d. Others, that all punishment under the righteous and benevolent government of God, must be disciplinary and remedial; and must finally result in the universal recovery of the lost to holiness and happiness;—

Finally, others believe, that while progress is the law of the soul, the eternal consequences of unfaithfulness here will be realized hereafter, in the consciously lower plane on which the unfaithful and impenitent must enter, and forever relatively continue, in "the world to come."

And now, in conclusion, let me say that this is probably the last time, in which I shall be called upon to discourse at such length, on those doctrines of the Gospel which are in controversy among its

* Luke 10 : 22.

followers. I have reached a period of life which, I had hoped, would save me from such discussions; but a period also, I would trust, when I could not be betrayed into that bitterness and asperity which is so apt to taint them as to have become proverbial. I yielded, however, the more readily to the request to prepare these Lectures, because on the one hand, I saw here and there efforts making, to revive and enforce an old and effete orthodoxy, the incubus of which the world had been by degrees throwing off; and on the other, to establish a cold and philosophic naturalism, which under the name and prestige of Liberal Christianity, seemed eating out its very life. For one, I know no Christianity, no Christian Unitarianism, without CHRIST; no Christ, except THE Christ of the New Testament; nor, for the sake of being thought or called, "*Liberal*"—that prefix which I once prized as much as any, but which has come to pander to and savor of "the vulgar love of license" far too much either for my taste or my convictions—will I consent to ignore or deny Him and his divine claims. If it be true, that in every free country there must be two great parties, in one or the other of which every man, who thinks at all, must assuredly find himself—"the parties of Progress and Conservatism; of those who (too often seem to) love the 'largest liberty' with more regard to its quantity than its quality, and those who desire only the best liberty, and dread as the greatest of evils, its corruption into license"—then is my position with the last, to live and to die. I see, I admit, however, no sole and inevitable alternative between these two great principles. Christianity, I am sure, is pre-eminently the Religion of Progress; but while it teaches us to "prove all things," it demands that we "hold fast that which is good." All speculation is not progress. Destructionism is not progress. God, who made the soul, has in the Gospel of his Son provided for and administered to its grand capacity for illimitable growth; and either to attempt to confine it in the swathing-bands of inexorable creeds, or to enlarge it by substituting a refined Deism for God's Revealed Truth—a system of mere Naturalism for that very Christianity to which all the while itself is indebted for whatever gives it any credence or worth—seems to me as preposterous as it is futile. If the last be progress at all, which I deny, it is progress in the wrong direction—"progress backwards."

Besides, another generation has reached maturity around me, demanding instruction on these subjects. Two objects, therefore, I have proposed to myself, in these Lectures. First, to save that Unitarianism, which I believe so well expresses the Christianity of Christ, from being confounded with erroneous opinions and views, which are too often in the community wrongfully identified with it, or baptized into its name; and next, to possess the minds and hearts of the children with a true knowledge and love of the holy and precious faith of their fathers; and thus give that faith to the best of my ability a fresh impulse in its onward course. Should the event prove that in any degree I have been successful, unto GOD be the praise!

GENERAL INDEX.

A

B

C

D

E

F

G

H

S

T

U

INDEX OF TEXTS.

Old Testament.

New Testament.

www.ingramcontent.com/pod-product-compliance
Lightning Source LLC
LaVergne TN
LVHW010236110826
845151LV00004B/1313
9781425524678